Good-Tasting, Happy Stomach

Your Way to Healthier Eating Habits

Jeffrey C. Stevenson

Cream of Rice Soup.

Two quarts of chicken stock (the water in which fowl have been boiled will answer), one tea-cupful of rice, a quart of cream or milk, a small onion, a stalk of celery and salt and pepper to taste. Wash rice carefully, and add to chicken stock, onion and celery. Cook slowly two hours (it should hardly bubble). Put through a sieve; add seasoning and the milk or cream, which has been allowed to come just to a boil. If milk, use also a table-spoonful of butter.

Cream of Barley Soup.

A tea-cupful of barley, well washed; three pints of chicken stock, an onion and a small piece each of mace and cinnamon. Cook slowly together five hours; then rub through a sieve, and add one and a half pints of boiling cream or milk. If milk, add also two table-spoonfuls of butter. Salt and pepper to taste. The yolks of four eggs, beaten with four table-spoonfuls of milk, and cooked a minute in the boiling milk or cream, makes the soup very much richer.

Duchess Soup.

One quart of milk, two large onions, three eggs, two table-spoonfuls of butter, two of flour, salt, pepper, two table-spoonfuls of grated cheese. Put milk on to boil. Fry the butter and onions together for eight minutes; then add dry flour, and cook two minutes longer, being careful not to burn. Stir into the milk, and cook ten minutes. Rub through a strainer, and return to the fire. Now add the cheese. Beat the eggs, with a speck of pepper and half a teaspoonful of salt. Season the soup with salt and pepper. Hold the colander over the soup and pour the eggs through, upon the butter, and set back for three minutes where it will not boll. Then serve. The cheese may be omitted if it is not liked.

Yacht Oyster Soup.

A quart of milk, one of oysters, a head of celery, a small onion, half a cupful of butter, half a cupful of powdered cracker, one teaspoonful of

Worcestershire sauce, a speck of cayenne and salt and pepper to taste. Chop onion and celery fine. Put on to boil with milk for twenty minutes. Then strain, and add the butter, cracker, oyster liquor, (which has been boiled and skimmed), and finally the seasoning and oysters. Cook three minutes longer, and serve.

LobsterSoupwithMilk.

Meat of a small lobster, chopped fine; three crackers, rolled fine, butter--size of an egg, salt and pepper to taste and a speck of cayenne. Mix all in the same pan, and add, gradually, a pint of boiling milk, stirring all the while. Boil up once, and serve.

LobsterSoupwithStock.

One small lobster, three pints of water or stock, three large table-spoonfuls of butter and three of flour, a speck of cayenne, white pepper and salt to taste. Break up the body of the lobster, and cut off the scraggy parts of the meat. Pour over these and the body the water or stock. If there is "coral" in the lobster, pound it and use also. Boil twenty minutes. Cook the butter and flour until smooth, but not brown. Stir into the cooking mixture and add the seasoning. Boil two minutes, and strain into a saucepan. Have the remainder of the lobster meat--that found in the tail and claws--cut up very fine, and add it to the soup. Boil up once, and serve.

PhiladelphiaClamSoup.

Twenty-five small clams, one quart of milk, half a cupful of butter, one table-spoonful of chopped parsley, three potatoes, two large table-spoonfuls of flour, salt, pepper. The clams should be chopped fine end put into a colander to drain. Pare the potatoes, and chop rather fine. Put them on to boil with the milk, in a double kettle. Rub the butter and flour together until perfectly creamy, and when the milk and potatoes have been boiling fifteen minutes, stir this in, and cook eight minutes more. Add the parsley, pepper and salt, and cook three minutes longer. Now add the clams. Cook one minute longer, and serve. This gives a very delicate soup, as the liquor from the clams is not used.

FishChowder.

Five pounds of any kind of fish, (the light salt-water fish is the best), half a pound of pork, two large onions, one quart of sliced potatoes, one quart of water, one pint of milk, two table-spoonfuls of flour, six crackers, salt, pepper. Skin the fish, and cut all the flesh from the bones. Put the bones onto cook in the quart of water, and simmer gently ten minutes. Fry the pork; then add the onions, cut into slices. Cover, and cook five minutes; then add the flour, and cook eight minutes longer, stirring often. Strain on this the water in which the fish bones were cooked and boil gently for five minutes; then strain all on the potatoes and fish. Season with salt and pepper, and simmer fifteen minutes. Add the milk and the crackers, which were first soaked for three minutes, in the milk. Let it boil up once, and serve. The milk maybe omitted, and a pint of tomatoes used, if you like.

CornChowder.

Cut enough green corn from the cob to make a quart; pare and slice one quart of potatoes; pare and slice two onions. Cut half a pound of pork in slices, and fry until brown then take up, and fry the onions in the fat. Put the potatoes and corn into the kettle in layers, sprinkling each layer with salt, pepper and flour. Use half a teaspoonful of pepper, one and a half table-spoonfuls of salt and three of flour. Place the gravy strainer on the vegetables, and turn the onions and pork fat into it, and with a spoon press the juice through; then slowly pour one and one-fourth quarts of boiling water through the strainer, rubbing as much onion through as possible. Take out the strainer, cover the kettle, and boil gently for twenty minutes. Mix three table-spoonfuls of flour with a little milk, and when perfectly smooth, add a pint and a half of rich milk. Stir this into the boiling chowder. Taste to see if seasoned enough, and if it is not, add more pepper and salt. Then add six crackers, split, and dipped for a minute in cold water. Put on the cover, boil up once, and serve.

CornSoup.

One pint of grated green com, one quart of milk, one pint of hot water, one heaping table-spoonful of flour, two table-spoonfuls of butter, one slice of onion, salt and pepper to taste. Cook the corn in the water thirty minutes.

Let the milk and onion come to a boil. Have the flour and butter mixed together, and add a few table-spoonfuls of the boiling milk. When perfectly smooth stir into the milk; and cook eight minutes. Take out the onion and add the corn. Season to taste, and serve.

Glaze.

Boil four quarts of consommé rapidly until reduced to one quart. Turn into small jars, and cool quickly. This will keep for a month in a cool, dry place. It is used for soups and sauces and for glazing meats.

FrenchPasteforSoups.

A preparation for flavoring and coloring soups and sauces comes in small tin boxes. In each box there are twelve little squares, which look very much like chocolate caramels. One of these will give two quarts of soup the most delicious flavor and a rich color. The paste should not be cooked with the soup, but put into the tureen, and the soup poured over it; and as the soup is served, stir with the ladle. If you let it boil with the clear soup the flavor will not be as fine and the soup not as clear. It may be used with any dark or clear soup, even when already seasoned. It is for sale in Boston by S.S. Pierce and McDewell & Adams; New York: Park, Tilford & Co., retail, E.C. Hayward & Co., 192-4 Chamber street, wholesale; Philadelphia: Githens & Rexsame's; Chicago: Rockwood Bros., 102 North Clark street; St. Louis: David Nicholson. The paste costs only twenty-five cents per box.

EggBalls.

Boil four eggs ten minutes. Drop into cold water, and when cool remove the yolks. Pound these in a mortar until reduced to a paste, and then beat them with a teaspoonful of salt, a speck of pepper and the white of one raw egg. Form in balls about the size of a walnut. Roll in flour, and fry brown in butter or chicken fat, being careful not to burn.

FriedBr eadforSoups.

Cut stale bread into dice, and fry in boiling fat until brown. It will take about half a minute. The fat must be smoking in the centre when the bread is put into it.

FISH.

A General Chapter on Fish.

It may seem as if a small number of recipes has been given, but the aim has been to present under the heads of Baking, Boiling, Broiling, Frying and Stewing such general directions that one cannot be at a loss as to how to prepare any kind of fish. Once having mastered the five primary methods, and learned also how to make sauces, the variety of dishes within the cook's power is great All that is required is confidence in the rules, which are perfectly reliable, and will always bring about a satisfactory result if followed carefully. Fish, to be eatable, should be perfectly fresh. Nothing else in the line of food deteriorates so rapidly, especially the white fish-those that are nearly free of oil, like cod, cusk, etc. Most of the oil in this class centres in the liver. Salmon, mackerel, etc., have it distributed throughout the body, which gives a higher and richer flavor, and at the same time tends to preserve the fish. People who do not live near the seashore do not get that delicious flavor which fish just caught have. If the fish is kept on ice until used, it will retain much of its freshness; let it once get heated and nothing will bring back the delicate flavor. Fresh fish will be firm, and the skin and scales bright. When fish looks dim and limp, do not buy it. Fish should be washed quickly in only one *(cold)* water, and should not be allowed to stand in it. If it is cut up before cooking, wash while whole, else much of the flavor will be lost. For frying, the fat should be deep enough to cover the article, and yet have it float from the bottom. Unless one cooks great quantities of fish in this way it is not necessary to have a separate pot of fat for this kind of frying. The same pot, with proper care, will answer for chops, cutlets, muffins, potatoes, croquettes, etc. All the cold fish left from any mode of cooking can be utilized in making delicious salads, croquettes, and escallops.

Boiled Fish.

A general role for boiling fish, which will hold good for all kinds, and thus save a great deal of time and space, is this: Any fresh fish weighing between four and six pounds should be first washed in cold water and then put into boiling water enough to cover it, and containing one table-spoonful of salt. Simmer gently thirty minutes; then take up. A fish kettle is a great convenience, and it can be used also for boiling hams. When you do not have a fish kettle, keep a piece of strong white cotton cloth in which pin the fish before putting into the boiling water. This will hold it in shape. Hard boiling will break the fish, and, of course, there will be great waste, besides the dish's not looking so handsome and appetizing. There should be a gentle bubbling of the water, and nothing more, all the time the fish is in it, A fish weighing more than six pounds should cook five minutes longer for every additional *two* pounds. Boiled fish can be served with a great variety of sauces. After you have learned to make them (which is a simple matter), if you cannot get a variety of fish you will not miss it particularly, the sauce and mode of serving doing much to change the whole character of the dish. Many people put a table-spoonful of vinegar in the water in which the fish is boiled. The fish flakes a little more readily for it. Small fish, like trout, require from four to eight minutes to cook. They are, however, much better baked, broiled or fried.

Court-Bouillon.

This preparation gives boiled fish a better flavor than cooking in clear water does. Many cooks use wine in it, but there is no necessity for it. Four quarts of water, one onion, one slice of carrot, two cloves, two table-spoonfuls of salt, one teaspoonful of pepper, one table-spoonful of vinegar, the juice of half a lemon and a bouquet of sweet herbs are used. Tie the onion, carrot, cloves and herbs in a piece of muslin, and put in the water with the other ingredients. Cover, and boil slowly for one hour. Then put in the fish and cook as directed for plain boiling.

BoiledCodwithLobsterSauce.

Boil the fish, as directed [see boiled fish], and, when done, carefully remove the skin from one side; then turn the fish over on to the dish on which it is to be served, skin side up. Remove the skin from this side. Wipe the dish with a damp cloth. Pour a few spoonfuls of the sauce over the fish, and the remainder around it; garnish with parsley, and serve. This is a handsome dish.

Boiled Haddock with Lobster Sauce.

The same as cod. In fact, all kinds of fish can be served in the same manner; but the lighter are the better, as the sauce is so rich that it is not really the thing for salmon and blue fish. Many of the best cooks and caterers, however, use the lobster sauce with salmon, but salmon has too rich and delicate a flavor to be mixed with the lobster.

Cold Boiled Fish, a la Vinaigrette.

If the fish is whole, take off the head and skin, and then place it in the centre of a dish. Have two cold hard-boiled eggs, and cut fine with a silver knife or spoon, (steel turns the egg black). Sprinkle the fish with this, and garnish either with small lettuce leaves, water-cresses, or cold boiled potatoes and beets, cut in slices. Place tastefully around the dish, with here and there a sprig of parsley. Serve the vinaigrette sauce in a separate dish. Help to the garnish when the fish is served, and pour a spoonful of the sauce over the fish as you serve it. This makes a nice dish for tea in summer, and takes the place of a salad, as it is, in fact, a kind of salad.

If the fish is left from the dinner, and is broken, pick free from skin and bones, heap it lightly in the centre of the dish, sprinkle the sauce over it, and set away in a cool place until tea time. Then add the garnish, and serve as before. Many people prefer the latter method, as the fish is seasoned better and more easily served. The cold fish remaining from a bake or broil can be served in the same manner. This same dish can be served with a sauce piquante or Tartare sauce, for a change.

Baked Fish.

As for the boiled fish, a general rule, that will cover all kinds of baked fish, is herewith given: A fish weighing about five pounds; three large, or five small, crackers, quarter of a pound of salt pork, two table-spoonfuls of salt, quarter of a teaspoonful of pepper, half a table-spoonful of chopped parsley, two table-spoonfuls of flour.

If the fish has not already been scraped free of scales, scrape, and wash clean; then rub into it one table-spoonful of the salt. Roll the crackers very fine, and add to them the parsley, one table-spoonful of chopped pork, half the pepper, half a table-spoonful of salt, and cold water to moisten well. Put this into the body of the fish, and fasten together with a skewer. Butter a tin sheet and put it into a baking pan. Cut gashes across the fish, about half an inch deep and two inches long. Cut the remainder of the pork into strips, and put these into the gashes. Now put the fish into the baking pan, and dredge well with salt, pepper and flour. Cover the bottom of the pan with hot water, and put into a rather hot oven. Bake one hour, basting often with the gravy in the pan, and dredging each time with salt, pepper and flour. The water in the pan must often be renewed, as the bottom is simply to be covered with it each time. The fish should be basted every fifteen minutes. When it is cooked, lift from the pan on to the tin sheet, and slide it carefully into the centre of the dish on which it is to be served. Pour around it Hollandaise sauce, tomato sauce, or any kind you like. Garnish with parsley.

BroiledFish.

Bluefish, young cod, mackerel, salmon, large trout, and all other fish, when they weigh between half a pound and four pounds, are nice for broiling. When smaller or larger they are not so good. Always use a double broiler, which, before putting the fish into it, rub with either butter or a piece of salt pork. This prevents sticking. The thickness of the fish will have to be the guide in broiling. A bluefish weighing four pounds will take from twenty minutes to half an hour to cook. Many cooks brown the fish handsomely over the coals and then put it into the oven to finish broiling. Where the fish is very thick, this is a good plan. If the fish is taken from the broiler to be put into the oven, it should be slipped on to a tin sheet, that it may slide easily into the platter at serving time; for nothing so mars a dish of fish as to have it come to the table broken. In broiling, the inside should be exposed to the fire first, and then the skin. Great care must be taken that the skin does not burn. Mackerel will broil in from twelve to twenty minutes, young cod (also called scrod) in from twenty to thirty minutes, bluefish in from twenty to thirty minutes, salmon, in from twelve to twenty minutes, and whitefish, bass, mullet, etc., in about eighteen minutes. All kinds of broiled fish can be served with a seasoning of salt, pepper and butter, or with any of the following sauces: *bearer noir, maître d' hôtel,* Tartare, sharp, tomato and curry. Always, when possible, garnish with parsley or something else green.

Broiled Halibut.

Season the slices with salt and pepper, and lay them in melted butter for half an hour, having them well covered on both sides. Roll in flour, and broil for twelve minutes over a clear fire. Serve on a hot dish, garnishing with parsley and slices of lemon. The slices of halibut should be about an inch thick, and for every pound there should be three table-spoonfuls of butter.

Broiled Halibut, with Maître d'Hôtel Butter.

Butter both sides of the broiler. Season the slices of halibut with salt and pepper, place them in the broiler and cook over clear coals for twelve minutes, turning frequently. Place on a hot dish, and spread on them the sauce, using one spoonful to each pound. Garnish with parsley.

Stewed Fish.

Six pounds of any kind of fish, large or small; three large pints of water, quarter of a pound of pork, or, half a cupful of butter; two large onions, three table-spoonfuls of flour, salt and pepper to taste. Cut the heads from the fish, and cut out all the bones. Put the heads and bones on to boil in the three pints of water. Cook gently half an hour. In the meanwhile cut the pork in slices, and fry brown. Cut the onions in slices, and fry in the pork fat. Stir the dry flour into the onion and fat, and cook three minutes, stirring all the time. Now pour over this the water in which the bones have been cooking, and simmer ten minutes. Have the fish cut in pieces about three inches square. Season well with salt and pepper, and place in the stew-pan. Season the sauce with salt and pepper, and strain on the fish. Cover tight, and simmer twenty minutes. A bouquet of sweet herbs, simmered with the bones, is an improvement. Taste to see if the sauce is seasoned enough, and dish on a large platter. Garnish with potato balls and parsley. The potato balls are cut from the raw potatoes with a vegetable scoop, and boiled ten minutes in salted water. Put them in little heaps around the dish.

Fried Fish.

All small fish, like brook trout, smelts, perch, etc., are best fried. They are often called pan-fish for this reason. They should be cleaned, washed and drained, then well salted, and rolled in flour and Indian meal (half of each), which has been thoroughly mixed and salted. For every four pounds of fish have half a pound of salt pork, cut in thin slices, and fried a crisp brown. Take the pork from the pan and put the fish in, having only enough to cover the bottom. Fry brown on one side; turn, and fry the other side. Serve on a hot dish, with the salt pork as a garnish. Great care must be taken that the pork or fat does not burn, and yet to have it hot enough to brown quickly. Cod, haddock, cusk and halibut are all cut in handsome slices and fried in this manner; or, the slices can be well seasoned with salt and pepper, dipped in beaten egg, rolled in bread or cracker crumbs and fried in boiling fat enough to cover. This method gives the handsomer dish, but the first the more savory. Where Indian meal is not liked, all flour can be used. Serve very hot Any kind of fried fish can be served with *beurre noir*, but this is particularly nice for that which is fried without pork. When the cooked fish is placed in the dish, pour the butter over it, garnish with parsley, and serve.

To Cook Salt Codfish.

The fish should be thoroughly washed, and soaked in cold water over night. In the morning change the water, and put on to cook. As soon as the water comes to the boiling point set back where it will keep *hot*, but will *not boil*. From four to six hours will cook a very dry, hard fish, and there are kinds which will cook in half an hour. The boneless codfish, put up at the Isles of Shoals, by Brown & Seavey, will cook in from half an hour to an hour. Where a family uses only a small quantity of salt fish at a time, this is a convenient and economical way to buy it, as there is no waste with bone or skin. It comes in five pound boxes, and costs sixty cents.

Dropped Fish Balls.

One pint bowlful of raw fish, two heaping bowlfuls of pared potatoes, (let the potatoes be under medium size), two eggs, butter, the size of an egg, and a little pepper. Pick the fish very fine, and measure it lightly in the bowl. Put the potatoes into the boiler, and the fish on top of them; then cover with boiling water, and boil half an hour. Drain off all the water, and mash fish and potatoes together until fine and light. Then add the butter and pepper, and the egg, well beaten. Have a deep kettle of *boiling* fat. Dip a tablespoon in it, and then take up a spoonful of the mixture, having care to get it into as good shape as possible. Drop into the boiling fat, and cook until brown, which should be in two minutes. Be careful not to crowd the balls, and, also, that the fat is hot enough. The spoon should be dipped in the fat every time you take a spoonful of the mixture. These balls are delicious.

Common Fish Balls.

One pint of finely-chopped cooked salt fish, six medium-sized potatoes, one egg, one heaping table-spoonful of butter, pepper, two table-spoonfuls of cream, or four of milk. Pare the potatoes, and put on in *boiling* water. Boil half an hour. Drain off all the water, turn the potatoes into the tray with the fish, and mash light and fine with a vegetable masher. Add the butter, pepper, milk and eggs, and mix all very thoroughly. Taste to see if salt enough. Shape into smooth balls, the size of an egg, and fry brown in boiling fat enough to float them. They will cook in three minutes. If the potatoes are very mealy it will take more milk or cream to moisten them, about two spoonfuls more. If the fat is smoking in the centre, and the balls are made *very* smooth, they will not soak fat; but if the fat is not hot enough, they certainly will. Putting too many balls into the fat at one time cools it. Put in say four or five. Let the fat regain its first temperature, then add more.

Salt Fish with Dropped Eggs.

One pint of cooked salt fish, one pint of milk or cream, two table-spoonfuls of flour, one of butter, six eggs, pepper. Put milk on to boil, keeping half a cupful of it to mix the flour. When it boils, stir in the flour, which has been mixed smooth with the milk; then add the fish, which has been flaked. Season, and cook ten minutes. Have six slices of toasted bread on a platter. Drop six eggs into boiling water, being careful to keep the shape. Turn the fish and cream on to the toast. Lift the eggs carefully from the water, as soon as the whites are set, and place very gently on the fish. Garnish the dish with points of toast and parsley.

Salt Codfish, in Purée of Potatoes.

Six large potatoes, one pint and one cupful of milk, two table-spoonfuls of butter, a small slice of onion (about the size of a silver quarter), one pint of cooked salt codfish, salt, pepper, one large table-spoonful of flour. Pare the potatoes and boil half an hour; then drain off the water, and mash them light and fine. Add the salt, pepper, one table-spoonful of butter, and the cupful of milk, which has been allowed to come to a boil. Beat very thoroughly, and spread a thin layer of the potatoes on the centre of a hot platter. Heap the remainder around the edge, making a wall to keep in the cream and fish, which should then be poured in. Garnish the border with parsley, and serve.

To prepare the fish: Put the pint of milk on to boil with the onion. Mix flour and butter together, and when well mixed, add two table-spoonfuls of the hot milk. Stir all into the boiling milk, skim out the onion, add the fish, and cook ten minutes. Season with pepper, and if not salty enough, with salt. This is a nice dish for breakfast, lunch or dinner.

Salt Fish Soufflé.

One pint of finely-chopped cooked salt fish, eight good-sized potatoes, three-fourths of a cupful of milk or cream, four eggs, salt, pepper, two generous table-spoonfuls of butter. Pare the potatoes and boil thirty minutes. Drain the water from them, and mash very fine; then mix thoroughly with the fish. Add butter, seasoning and the hot milk. Have two of the eggs well beaten, which stir into the mixture, and heap this in the dish in which it is to be served. Place in the oven for ten minutes. Beat the whites of the two remaining eggs to a stiff froth, and add a quarter of a teaspoonful of salt; then add yolks. Spread this over the dish of fish; return to the oven to brown, and serve.

Cusk, à la Crème.

A cusk, cod or haddock, weighing five or six pounds; one quart of milk, two table-spoonfuls of flour, one of butter, one small slice of onion, two sprigs of parsley, salt, pepper. Put the fish on in boiling water enough to cover, and which contains one table-spoonful of salt. Cook gently twenty minutes; then lift out of the water, but let it remain on the tray. Now carefully remove all the skin and the head; then turn the fish over into the dish in which it is to be served (it should be stone china), and scrape off the skin from the other side. Pick out all the small bones. You will find them the whole length of the back, and a few in the lower part of the fish, near the tail. They are in rows like pins in a paper, and if you start all right it will take but a few minutes to remove them. Then take out the back-bone, starting at the head and working gently down toward the tail. Great care must be taken, that the fish may keep its shape. Cover with the cream, and bake about ten minutes, just to brown it a little. Garnish with parsley or little puff-paste cakes; or, you can cover it with the whites of three eggs, beaten to a stiff froth, and then slightly brown.

To prepare the cream: Put the milk, parsley and onion on to boil, reserving half a cupful of milk to mix with the flour. When it boils, stir in the flour, which has been mixed smoothly with the cold milk. Cook eight minutes. Season highly with salt and pepper, add the butter, strain on the fish, and proceed as directed.

EscalopedFish.

One pint of milk, one pint of cream, four table-spoonfuls of flour, one cupful of bread crumbs and between four and five pounds of any kind of white fish--cusk, cod, haddock, etc., boiled twenty minutes in water to cover and two table-spoonfuls of salt. Put fish on to boil, then the cream and milk. Mix the flour with half a cupful of cold milk, and stir into boiling cream and milk. Cook eight minutes and season highly with salt and pepper. Remove skin and bones from fish, and break it into flakes. Put a layer of sauce in a deep escalop dish, and then a layer of fish, which dredge well with salt (a table-spoonful) and pepper; then another layer of sauce, again fish, and then sauce. Cover with the bread crumbs, and bake half an hour. This quantity requires a dish holding a little over two quarts, or, two smaller dishes will answer. If for the only solid dish for dinner, this will answer for six persons; but if it is in a course for a dinner party, it will serve twelve. Cold boiled fish can be used when you have it. Great care must be taken to remove every bone when fish is prepared with a sauce, (as when it is served *à la crème*, escaloped, &c.), because one cannot look for bones then as when the sauce is served separately.

Turbot à la Crème.

Boil five or six pounds of haddock. Take out all bones, and shred the fish very fine. Let a quart of milk, a quarter of an onion and a piece of parsley come to a boil; then stir in a scant cupful of flour, which has been mixed with a cupful of cold milk, and the yolks of two eggs. Season with half a teaspoonful of white pepper, the same quantity of thyme, half a cupful of butter, and well with salt. Butter a pan, and put in first a layer of sauce, then one of fish. Finish with sauce, and over it sprinkle cracker crumbs and a light grating of cheese. Bake for an hour in a moderate oven.

Matelote of Codfish.

Cut off the head of a codfish weighing five pounds. Remove bones from the fish, and fill it with a dressing made of half a pint of oysters, a scant pint of bread crumbs, a fourth of a teaspoonful of pepper, two teaspoonfuls of salt, two table-spoonfuls of butter, half an onion, an egg and half a table-spoonful of chopped parsley. Place five slices of pork both under and over the fish. Boil the bones in a pint of water, and pour this around the fish. Bake an hour, and baste often with gravy and butter. Have a bouquet in the corner of the baking pan. Make a gravy, and pour around the fish. Then garnish with fried smelts.

Smelts à la Tartare.

Clean the smelts by drawing them between the finger and thumb, beginning at the tail. This will press out the insides at the opening at the gills. Wash them, and drain in the colander; salt well, and dip in beaten egg and bread or cracker crumbs (one egg and one cupful of crumbs to twelve smelts, unless these are very large). Dip first in the egg, and then roll in the crumbs. Fry in boiling fat deep enough to float them. They should be a handsome brown in two minutes and a half. Take them up, and place on a sheet of brown paper for a few moments, to drain; then place on a hot dish. Garnish with parsley and a few slices of lemon, and serve with Tartare sauce in a separate dish; or, they may be served without the sauce.

Smelts as a Garnish,

Smelts are often fried, as for *à la Tartare*; or, rolled in meal or flour, and then fried, they are used to garnish other kinds of fish. With baked fish they are arranged around the dish in any form that the taste of the cook may dictate; but in garnishing fish, or any other dish, the arrangement should always be simple, so as not to make the matter of serving any harder than if the dish were not garnished. Smelts are also seasoned well with salt and pepper, dipped in butter and afterwards in flour, and placed in a very hot oven for eight or ten minutes to get a handsome brown. They are then served as a garnish or on slices of buttered toast. When smelts are used as a garnish, serve one on each plate with the other fish. If you wish to have the smelts in rings, for a garnish, fasten the tails in the opening at the gills, with little wooden tooth picks; then dip them in the beaten egg and in the crumbs, place in the frying basket and plunge into the boiling fat. When they are cooked take out the skewers, and they will retain their shape.

FishauGratin .

Any kind of light fish--that is, cod, cusk, flounder, etc. Skin the fish by starting at the head and drawing down towards the tail; then take out the bones. Cut the fish into pieces about three inches square, and salt and pepper well. Butter such a dish, as you would use for escolloped oysters. Put in one layer of fish, then moisten well with sauce; add more fish and sauce, and finally cover with fine bread crumbs. Bake half an hour. The dish should be rather shallow, allowing only two layers of fish.

Sauce for *au gratin*: One pint of stock, three table-spoonfuls of butter, two of flour, juice of half a lemon, half a table-spoonful of chopped parsley, a slice of onion, the size of half a dollar, and about as thick--chopped very fine, (one table-spoonful of onion juice is better); one table-spoonful of vinegar, salt, pepper. Heat the butter in a small frying-pan, and when hot, add the dry flour. Stir constantly until a rich brown; then add, gradually, the cold stock, stirring all the time. As soon as it boils, season well with salt and pepper, and then add the other seasoning. This quantity is enough for three pounds of fish, weighed after being skinned and boned, and will serve six persons if it is the only solid dish for dinner, or ten if served in a course.

Another way to serve fish *au gratin,* is to skin it, cut off the head, and take out the back-bone; and there are then two large pieces of fish. Season the fish, and prepare the sauce as before. Butter a tin sheet that will fit loosely into a large baking-pan. Lay the fish on this, and moisten well with the sauce. Cover thickly with bread crumbs, and cook twenty-five minutes in a rather quick oven. Then slip on a hot dish, and serve with tomato, Tartare or Hollandaise sauce poured around the fish.

Eels à la Tartare.

Cut the eels into pieces about four inches long. Cover them with boiling water, in which let them stand five minutes, and then drain them. Now dip in beaten egg, which has been well salted and peppered, then in bread or cracker crumbs. Fry in boiling fat for five minutes. Have Tartare sauce spread in the centre of a cold dish. Place the fried eels in a circle on this, garnish with parsley, and serve.

Stewed Eels.

Cut two eels in pieces about four inches long. Put three large table-spoonfuls of butter into the stew-pan with half a small onion. As soon as the onion begins to turn yellow stir in two table-spoonfuls of flour, and stir until brown. Add one pint of stock, if you have it; if not, use water. Season well with pepper and salt; then put in the eels and two bay leaves. Cover, and simmer gently three-quarters of an hour. Heap the eels in the centre of a hot dish, strain the sauce over them and garnish with toasted bread and parsley. If you wish, add a table-spoonful of vinegar or lemon juice to the stew.

OYSTERS.

On the Half Shell.

Not until just before serving should they be opened. Marketmen often furnish some one to do this. Six large oysters are usually allowed each person. Left in half the shell, they are placed on a dinner plate, with a thin slice of lemon in the centre of the dish.

On a Block of Ice.

Having a perfectly clear and solid block of ice, weighing ten or fifteen pounds, a cavity is to be made in the top of it in either of two ways. The first is to carefully chip with an ice pick; the other, to melt with heated bricks. If the latter be chosen the ice must be put into a tub or large pan, and one of the bricks held upon the centre of it until there is a slight depression, yet sufficient for the brick to rest in. When the first brick is cold remove it, tip the block on one side, to let off the water, and then use another brick. Continue the operation till the cavity will hold as many oysters as are to be served. These should be kept an hour previous in a cool place; should be drained in a colander, and seasoned with salt, pepper and vinegar. After laying two folded napkins on a large platter, to prevent the block from slipping, cover the dish with parsley, so that only the ice is visible. Stick a number of pinks, or of any small, bright flowers that do not wilt rapidly, into the parsley. Pour oysters into the space in the top of the ice, and garnish with thin slices of lemon. This gives an elegant dish, and does away with the unsightly shells in which raw oysters are usually served. It is not expensive, for the common oysters do as well as those of good size. Indeed, as many ladies dislike the large ones, here is an excellent substitute for serving in the shell, particularly as the oysters require no seasoning when once on the table. A quart is enough for a party of ten; but a block of the size given will hold two quarts.

Roasted Oysters on Toast.

Eighteen large oysters, or thirty small ones, one teaspoonful of flour, one table-spoonful of butter, salt, pepper, three slices of toast. Have the toast buttered and on a hot dish. Put the butter in a small sauce-pan, and when hot, add the dry flour. Stir until smooth, but not brown; then add the cream, and let it boil up once. Put the oysters (in their own liquor) into a hot oven, for three minutes; then add them to the cream. Season, and pour over the toast. Garnish the dish with thin slices of lemon, and serve very hot. It is nice for lunch or tea.

OystersPannedintheirOwnLiquor .

Eighteen large, or thirty small, oysters, one table-spoonful of butter, one of cracker crumbs, salt and pepper to taste, one teaspoonful of lemon juice, a speck of cayenne. Put the oysters on in their own liquor, and when they boil up, add seasoning, butter and crumbs. Cook one minute, and serve on toast.

OystersPannedintheShell.

Wash the shells and wipe dry. Place them in a pan with the round shell down. Set in a hot oven for three minutes; then take out, and remove the upper shell. Put two or three oysters into one of the round shells, season with pepper and salt, add butter, the size of two peas, and cover with cracker or bread crumbs. Return to the oven and brown.

OysterSauté.

Two dozen large, or three dozen small, oysters, two table-spoonfuls of butter, four of fine cracker crumbs, salt, pepper. Let the oysters drain in the colander. Then season with salt and pepper and roll in the crumbs. Have the butter very hot in a frying-pan, and put in enough of the oysters to cover the bottom of the pan. Fry crisp and brown, being careful not to burn. Serve on hot, crisp toast.

OystersRoastedintheShell.

Wash the shells clean, and wipe dry. Place in a baking pan, and put in a hot oven for about twenty minutes. Serve on hot dishes the moment they are taken from the oven. Though this is not an elegant dish, many people enjoy it, as the first and best flavor of the oysters is retained in this manner of cooking. The oysters can, instead, be opened into a hot dish and seasoned with butter, salt, pepper and lemon juice. They should be served immediately.

LittlePigsinBlankets.

Season large oysters with salt and pepper. Cut fat English bacon in very thin slices, wrap an oyster in each slice, and fasten with a little wooden skewer (toothpicks are the best things). Heat a frying-pan and put in the "little pigs." Cook just long enough to crisp the bacon--about two minutes. Place on slices of toast that have been cut into small pieces, and serve immediately. Do not remove the skewers. This is a nice relish for lunch or tea; and, garnished with parsley, is a pretty one. The pan must be very hot before the "pigs" are put in, and then great care must be taken that they do not burn.

Fricasseed Oysters.

One hundred oysters (about two quarts), four large table-spoonfuls of butter, one teaspoonful of chopped parsley, one table-spoonful of flour, a speck of cayenne, salt, yolks of three eggs. Brown two table-spoonfuls of the butter, and add to it the parsley, cayenne and salt and the oysters, well drained. Mix together the flour and the remainder of the butter and stir into the oysters when they begin to curl. Then add yolks, well beaten, and take immediately from the fire. Serve on a hot dish with a garnish of fried bread and parsley.

Creamed Oysters.

A pint of cream, one quart of oysters, a small piece of onion, a very small piece of mace, a table-spoonful of flour, and salt and pepper to taste. Let the cream, with the onion and mace, come to a boil. Mix flour with a little cold milk or cream, and stir into the boiling cream. Let the oysters come to a boil in their own liquor, and skim carefully. Drain off all the liquor, and turn the oysters into the cream. Skim out the mace and onions, and serve.

Crôustade of Oysters .

Have a loaf of bread baked in a round two-quart basin. When two or three days old, with a sharp knife cut out the heart of the bread, being careful not to break the crust. Break up the crumbs very fine, and dry them slowly in an oven; then quickly fry three cupfuls of them in two table-spoonfuls of butter. As soon as they begin to look golden and are crisp, they are done. It takes about two minutes over a hot fire, stirring all the time. Put one quart of cream to boil, and when it boils, stir in three table-spoonfuls of flour, which has been mixed with half a cupful of cold milk. Cook eight minutes. Season well with salt and pepper. Put a layer of the sauce into the *crôustade* then a layer of oysters, which dredge well with salt and pepper; then another layer of sauce and one of fried crumbs. Continue this until the *crôustade* is nearly full, having the last layer a thick one of crumbs. It takes three pints of oysters for this dish, and about three teaspoonfuls of salt and half a teaspoonful of pepper. Bake slowly half an hour. Serve with a garnish of parsley around the dish,

EscalopedOysters.

Two quarts of oysters, half a cupful of butter, half a cupful of cream or milk, four teaspoonfuls of salt, half a teaspoonful of pepper, two quarts of stale bread crumbs, and spice, if you choose. Butter the escalop dishes, and put in a layer of crumbs and then one of oysters. Dredge with the salt and pepper, and put small pieces of butter here and there in the dish. Now have another layer of oysters, seasoning as before; then add the milk, and, finally, a thick layer of crumbs, which dot with butter. Bake twenty minutes in a rather quick oven. The crumbs must be light and flakey. The quantity given above is enough to fill two dishes.

EscalopedOysters,No.2.

Put a layer of rolled crackers in an oval dish, and then a layer of oysters, and lay on small pieces of butter. Dredge with salt and pepper, and moisten well with milk (or equal parts of milk and water). Add another layer of cracker and of oysters, and butter, dredge and moisten as before. Continue these alternate layers until the dish is nearly full; then cover with a thin layer of cracker and pieces of butter. If the dish be a large one, holding about two quarts, it will require an hour and a half or two hours to bake.

OystersServedinEscalopShells.

The shells may be tin, granite-ware, or silver-plated, or, the natural oyster or scollop shells. The ingredients are: one quart of oysters, half a pint of cream or milk, one pint of bread crumbs, one table-spoonful of butter, if cream is used, or three, if milk; salt and pepper, a grating of nutmeg and two table-spoonfuls of flour. Drain all the liquor from the oysters into a stew-pan. Let it come to a boil, and skim; then add the cream or milk, with which the flour should first be mixed. Let this boil two minutes, and add the butter, salt, pepper and nutmeg, and then the oysters. Take from the fire immediately. Taste to see if seasoned enough. Have the shells buttered, and sprinkled lightly with crumbs. Nearly fill them with the prepared oysters;

then cover thickly with crumbs. Put the shells in a baking-pan, and bake fifteen minutes. Serve very hot, on a large platter, which garnish with parsley. The quantity given above will fill twelve common-sized shells.

OysterChartr euse.

One quart of oysters, one pint of cream, one small slice of onion, half a cupful of milk, whites of four eggs, two table-spoonfuls of butter, salt, pepper, two table-spoonfuls of flour, one cupful of fine, dry bread crumbs, six potatoes. Pare and boil the potatoes. Mash fine and light, and add the milk, salt, pepper, one spoonful of butter, and then the whites of the eggs, beaten to a stiff froth. Have a two-quart charlotte russe mould well buttered, and sprinkle the bottom and sides with the bread crumbs (there must be butter enough to hold the crumbs). Line the mould with the potato, and let stand for a few minutes. Put the cream and onion on to boil. Mix the flour with a little cold milk or cream--about one-fourth of a cupful--and stir into the boiling cream. Season well with salt and pepper, and cook eight minutes. Let the oysters come to a boil in their own liquor. Skim them, and drain of all the juice. Take the piece of onion from the sauce, and add the oysters. Taste to see if seasoned enough, and turn gently into the mould. Cover with the remainder of the potato, being careful not to put on too much at once, as in that case the sauce would be forced to the top. When covered, bake half an hour in a hot oven. Take from the oven ten minutes before dishing time, and let it stand on the table. Place a large platter over the mould and turn both dish and mould at the same time. Remove the mould very gently. Garnish the dish with parsley, and serve. A word of caution: Every part of the mould must have a thick coating of the mashed potato, and when the covering of potato is put on no opening must be left for sauce to escape.

ToPickleOysters .

Two hundred large oysters, half a pint of vinegar, half a pint of white wine, four spoonfuls of salt, six spoonfuls of whole black pepper and a little mace. Strain the liquor, and add the above-named ingredients. Let boil up once, and pour, while boiling hot, over the oysters. After these have stood ten minutes pour off the liquor, which, as well as the oysters, should then be allowed to get cold. Put into a jar and cover tight. The oysters will keep some time.

LOBSTER.

Lobster, to be eatable, should be perfectly fresh. One of the tests of freshness is to draw back the tail, for if it springs into position again, it is safe to think the fish good. The time of boiling varies with the size of the lobster and in different localities. In Boston, Rockport and other places on the Massachusetts coast the time is fifteen or twenty minutes for large lobsters and ten for small. The usual way is to plunge them into boiling water enough to cover, and to continue boiling them until they are done. Some people advocate putting the lobsters into cold water, and letting this come to a boil gradually. They claim that the lobsters do not suffer so much. This may be so, but it seems as if death must instantly follow the plunge into boiling water. Cooking a lobster too long makes it tough and dry. When, on opening a lobster, you find the meat clinging to the shell, and very much shrunken, you may be sure the time of boiling was too long. There are very few modes of cooking lobster in which it should be more than thoroughly heated, as much cooking toughens it and destroys the fine, delicate flavor of the meat.

Toopenalobster .

Separate the tail from the body, and shake out the tom-ally, and, also, the "coral," if there is any, upon a plate. Then by drawing the body from the shell with the thumb, and pressing the part near the head against the shell with the first and second finger, you will free it from the stomach or "lady." Now split the lobster through the centre and, with a fork, pick the meat from the joints. Cut the under side of the tail shell open and take out the meat without breaking. On the upper part of that end of this meat which joined the body is a small piece of flesh, which should be lifted; and a strip of meat attached to it should be turned back to the extreme end of the tail. This will uncover a little vein, running the entire length, which must be removed. Sometimes this vein is dark, and sometimes as light as the meat itself. It and the stomach are the only parts not eatable. The piece that covered the vein should be turned again into place. Hold the claws on edge on a thick board, and strike hard with a hammer until the shell cracks. Draw apart, and take out the meat. If you have the claws lying flat on the board when you strike, you not only break the shell, but mash the meat, and thus spoil a fine dish. Remember that the stomach of the lobster is found near the head, and is a small, hard sack containing poisonous matter; and that the intestinal vein is found in the tail. These should always be carefully removed. When lobster is opened in the manner explained it may be arranged handsomely on a dish, and each person can season it at the table to suit himself.

Lobster Broiled in the Shell.

Divide the tail into two parts, cutting lengthwise. Break the large claws in two parts, and free the body from the small claws and stomach. Replace the body in the shell. Put the meat from the claws in half of the shells it came from, and put the other half of the shells where they will get hot. Put the lobster into the double broiler, and cook, with the meat side exposed to the fire, for eight minutes; then turn, and cook ten minutes longer. Place on a hot dish, and season slightly with salt and cayenne, and then well with *maître d' hôtel* butter. Cover the claws with the hot shells. Garnish the dish with parsley, and serve.

Broiled Lobster.

Split the meat of the tail and claws, and season well with salt and pepper. Cover with soft butter and dredge with flour. Place in the broiler, and cook over a bright fire until a delicate brown. Arrange on a hot dish, pour Bechamel sauce around, and serve.

Breaded Lobster.

Split the meat of the tail and claws, and season well with salt and pepper. Dip in beaten egg and then in bread crumbs, which let dry on the meat; and then repeat the operation. Place in a frying-basket, and plunge into boiling fat. Cook till a golden brown--about two minutes. Serve with Tartare sauce.

Stewed Lobster.

The meat of a two and a half pound lobster, cut into dice; two table-spoonfuls of butter, two of flour, one pint of stock or water, a speck of cayenne, salt and pepper to taste. Let the butter get hot, and add the dry flour. Stir until perfectly smooth, when add the water, gradually, stirring all the while. Season to taste. Add the lobster; heat thoroughly, and serve.

Curry of Lobster .

The meat of a lobster weighing between two and three pounds, one very small onion, three table-spoonfuls of butter, two of flour, a scant one of curry powder, a speck of cayenne, salt, a scant pint of water or stock. Let the butter get hot; and then add the onion, cut fine, and fry brown. When the onion is cooked add the flour and curry powder, and stir all together for two minutes. Add stock; cook two minutes, and strain. Add the meat of lobster, cut into dice, and simmer five minutes. Serve with a border of boiled rice around the dish.

Devilled Lobster in the Shell.

Two lobsters, each weighing about two and a half pounds; one pint of cream, two table-spoonfuls of butter, two of flour, one of mustard, a speck of cayenne, salt, pepper, a scant pint of bread crumbs. Open the lobster and, with a sharp knife, cut the meat rather fine. Be careful, in opening, not to break the body or tail shells. Wash these shells and wipe dry; join them in the form of a boat, that they may hold the prepared meat. Put the cream on to boil. Mix the butter, flour, mustard and pepper together, and add three spoonfuls of the boiling cream. Stir all into the remaining cream, and cook two minutes. Add the lobster, salt and pepper, and boil one minute. Fill the shells with the mixture, and place in a pan, with something to keep them in position (a few small stones answer very well). Cover with the bread crumbs, and brown for twenty minutes in a hot oven. Serve on a long, narrow dish; the body in the centre, the tails at either end. Garnish with parsley. If for a large company, it would be best to have a broad dish, and have four lobsters, instead of two. This is a very handsome dish, and is really not hard to cook. There is always a little more of the prepared lobster than will go into the shells without crowding, and this is nice warmed and served on slices of crisp toast.

Escaloped Lobster.

Prepare the lobster as for devilling, omitting, however, the mustard. Turn into a buttered escollop dish, and cover thickly with crumbs. Brown in a hot oven, and serve.

White stock may be used instead of the cream. Many people who cannot eat lobster when prepared with cream or milk, find it palatable when prepared with stock or water.

Lobster Cutlets.

A lobster weighing between two and a half and three pounds, three tablespoonfuls of butter, half a cupful of stock or cream, one heaping tablespoonful of flour, a speck of cayenne, salt, two eggs, about a pint of bread crumbs, twelve sprigs of parsley. Cut the meat of the lobster into fine dice, and season with salt and pepper. Put the butter on to heat. Add the flour, and when smooth, add the stock and one well-beaten egg. Season. Boil up once, add the lobster, and take from the fire immediately. Now add a tablespoonful of lemon juice. Butter a platter, and pour the mixture upon it, to the thickness of about an inch. Make perfectly smooth with a knife, and set away to cool. When cool, cut into chops, to resemble cutlets. Dip in beaten egg and then in bread crumbs, being sure to have every part covered. Place in the frying-basket and plunge into boiling fat. Cook till a rich brown. It will take about two minutes. Drain for a moment in the basket; then arrange on a hot dish, and put part of a small claw in each one, to represent the bone in a cutlet. Put the parsley in the basket and plunge for a moment into the boiling fat. Garnish with this, or, pour a white or Bechamel sauce around the dish, and garnish with fresh parsley. The quantity given will make six or seven cutlets.

Canned Lobster.

Canned lobster can be used for cutlets, stews, curries and patties, can be escaloped, or served on toast.

OTHER SHELL-FISH.

Stewed Terrapins.

Put them into boiling water, and boil rapidly for ten or fifteen minutes, or until the nails will come out and the black skin rub off--the time depending upon the size of the fish. After this, put into fresh boiling water, and boil until the under shell cracks, which will be about three-quarters of an hour. Remove the under shell, throw away the sand and gall bags, take out intestines, and put the terrapins to boil again in the same water for an hour. Pick liver and meat from upper shell. Cut the intestines in small pieces, and add to this meat. Pour over all a quantity of the liquor in which the intestines were boiled sufficient to make very moist. Put away until the next day. For each terrapin, if of good size, a gill of cream and of wine, half a cupful of butter, yolks of two hard-boiled eggs, rubbed smooth, salt, pepper and cayenne are needed. Pour over the terrapin, let it come to a boil, and serve,--[Mrs. Furness, of Philadelphia.]

Soft-Shell Crabs.

Lift the shell at both sides and remove the spongy substance found on the back. Then pull off the "apron," which will be found on the under side, and to which is attached a substance like that removed from the back. Now wipe the crabs, and dip them in beaten egg, and then in fine bread or cracker crumbs. Fry in boiling fat from eight to ten minutes, the time depending upon the size of the crabs. Serve with Tartare sauce. Or, the egg and bread crumbs may be omitted. Season with salt and cayenne, and fry as before,

When broiled, crabs are cleaned, and seasoned with salt and cayenne; are then dropped into boiling water for one minute, taken up, and broiled over a hot fire for eight minutes. They are served with *maître d' hôtel* butter or Tartare sauce.

MEATS.

BOILING.

All pieces, unless very salt, should be plunged into boiling water, and boiled rapidly for fifteen minutes, to harden the albumen that is on the outside, and thus keep in the juices. The kettle should then be put back where it will just simmer, for meat that is boiled rapidly becomes hard and stringy, while that which is kept just at the boiling point (where the water hardly bubbles) will cut tender and juicy, provided there is any juiciness in it at the beginning. White meats, like mutton and poultry, are improved in appearance by having rice boiled with them; or, a still better way is to thickly flour a piece of coarse cotton cloth, pin the meat in it, and place in the boiling water. Meat cooked in this way will be extremely juicy.

Leg of Mutton.

Cook, as directed, in boiling water to cover. A leg that weighs eight or nine pounds will cook in one hour and a quarter if it is wanted done rare. Allow five minutes for every additional pound. Save the water for soups.

Lamb.

Cook the same as mutton. Serve with drawn butter.

Boiled Ham.

Wash the ham very clean, and put on with cold water to cover. Simmer gently five hours, and set the kettle aside for one or two hours. When nearly cold, take out the ham and draw off the skin. Cover with cracker crumbs and about three table-spoonfuls of sugar. Place in the oven, in a baking-pan, for thirty or forty minutes. Many people stick cloves into the fat part of the ham, and use only a few crumbs. The time given is for a ham weighing about twelve pounds; every pound over that will require fifteen minutes more. The fish kettle comes next to a regular ham kettle, and answers quite as well as both. If you have neither kettle, and no pot large enough to hold all the meat, cut off the knuckle, which will cook in about two hours. But this rather hurts the flavor and appearance of the dish.

Salt Tongue.

Soak over night, and cook from five to six hours. Throw into cold water and peel off the skin.

FreshTongue.

Put into boiling water to cover, with two table-spoonfuls of salt. Cook from five to six hours. Skin the same as salt tongue.

CornedBeef.

Wash, and put into cold water, if very salt; but such a piece as one finds in town and city shops, and which the butchers corn themselves, put into boiling water. Cook very slowly for six hours. This time is for a piece weighing eight or ten pounds. When it is to be served cold let it stand for one or two hours in the water in which it was boiled. If the beef is to be pressed, get either a piece of the brisket, flank or rattle-ran. Take out the bones, place in a flat dish or platter, put a tin sheet on top, and lay on it two or three bricks. If you have a corned beef press, use that, of course.

ROASTING.

There are two modes of roasting: one is to use a tin Kitchen before an open fire, and the other and more common way is to use a very hot oven. The former gives the more delicious favor, but the second is not by any means a poor way, if the meat is put on a rack, and basted constantly when in the oven. A large piece is best for roasting, this being especially true of beef. When meat is cooked in a tin kitchen it requires more time, because the heat is not equally distributed, as it is in the oven.

To prepare for roasting: Wipe the meat with a wet towel. Dredge on all sides with salt, pepper and flour; and if the kitchen is used, dredge the flour into that. Run the spit through the centre of the meat, and place very near the fire at first, turning as it browns. When the flour in the kitchen is browned, add a pint of hot water, and baste frequently with it, dredging with salt and flour after each basting. Roast a piece of beef weighing eight pounds fifty minutes, if to be rare, but if to be medium, roast one hour and a quarter, and ten minutes for each additional pound.

Roasting in the Oven.

Prepare the meat as before. Have a rack that will fit loosely into the baking-pan. Cover the bottom of the pan rather lightly with flour, put in rack, and then meat Place in a very hot oven for a few minutes, to brown the flour in the pan, and then add hot water enough to cover the bottom of the pan. Close the oven; and in about ten minutes, open, and baste the meat with the gravy. Dredge with salt, pepper and flour. Do this every fifteen minutes; and as soon as one side of the meat is brown, turn, and brown the other. Make gravy as before. Allow a quarter of an hour less in the oven than in the tin kitchen. The heat for roasting must be very great at first, to harden the albumen, and thus keep in the juices. After the meat is crusted over it is not necessary to keep up so great a heat, but for rare meats the heat must, of course, be greater than for those that are to be well done. The kitchen can be drawn back a little distance from the fire and the drafts closed. Putting salt on fresh meat draws out the juices, but by using flour a paste is formed, which, keeps in all the juices and also enriches and browns the piece. Never roast meat without having a rack in the pan. If meat is put into the water in the pan it becomes soggy and looses its flavor. A meat rack costs not more than thirty or forty cents, and the improvement in the looks and flavor of a piece of meat is enough to pay for it in one roasting. The time given for roasting a piece of beef is for rib roasts and sirloin. The same weight in the face or the back of the rump will require twenty minutes longer, as the meat on these cuts is in a very compact form. If a saddle or loin of mutton is to be roasted, cook the same time as beef if the weight is the same; but if a leg is to be roasted, one hour and a quarter is the time. Lamb should be cooked an hour and a half; veal, two hours and three-quarters; pork, three hours and a quarter. Ten minutes before dishing the dinner turn the gravy into a sauce-pan, skim off all the fat, and set on the stove. Let it come to a boil; then stir in one table-spoonful of flour, mixed with half a cupful of cold water. Season with salt and pepper, and cook two minutes. Serve the meat on a hot dish and the gravy in a hot tureen.

Boiled Rib Roast.

Either have the butcher remove the bones, or do it your-self by slipping a sharp knife between the flesh and bones--a simple matter with almost any kind of meat. Roll up the piece and tie with strong twine. Treat the same as plain roast beef, giving the same time as if it were a piece of rump (one hour and a half for eight pounds), as the form it is now in does not readily admit the heat to all parts. This piece of beef can be larded before roasting, or it can be larded and braised. Serve with tomato or horse-radish sauce.

Roast Beef, with Yorkshire Pudding.

A rib or sirloin roast should be prepared as directed for roasting. When within three-quarters of an hour of being done, have the pudding made. Butter a pan like that in which the meat is being cooked, and pour in the batter. Put the rack across the pan, not in it. Place the meat on the rack, return to the oven, and cook forty-five minutes. If you have only one pan, take up the meat, pour off the gravy and put in the pudding. Cut in squares, and garnish the beef with these. Another method is to have a pan that has squares stamped in it. This gives even squares and crust on all the edges, which baking in the flat pan does not. When the meat is roasted in the tin-kitchen, let the pudding bake in the oven for half an hour, and then place it under the meat to catch the drippings.

For the Yorkshire pudding, one pint of milk, two-thirds of a cupful of flour, three eggs and one scant teaspoonful of salt will be needed. Beat the eggs very light. Add salt and milk, and then pour about half a cupful of the mixture upon the flour; and when perfectly smooth, add the remainder. This makes a small pudding--about enough for six persons. Serve it hot.

Fillet of Veal, Roasted.

About eight or ten pounds of the fillet, ham force-meat (see rule for force-meat), half a cupful of butter, half a teaspoonful of pepper, two table-spoonfuls of salt, two lemons, half a pound of salt pork. Rub the salt and pepper into the veal; then fill the cavity, from which the bone was taken, with the force-meat. Skewer and tie the fillet into a round shape. Cut the pork in thin slices, and put half of these on a tin sheet that will fit into the dripping pan; place this in the pan, and the fillet on it. Cover the veal with the remainder of the pork. Put hot water enough in the pan to just cover the bottom, and place in the oven. Bake slowly for four hours, basting frequently with the gravy in the pan, and with salt, pepper and flour. As the water in the pan cooks away, it must be renewed, remembering to have only enough to keep the meat and pan from burning. After it has been cooking three hours, take the pork from the top of the fillet, spread the top thickly with butter and dredge with flour. Repeat this after thirty minutes, and then brown handsomely. Put the remainder of the butter, which should be about three table-spoonfuls, in a sauce-pan, and when hot, add two heaping table-spoonfuls of flour, and stir until dark brown. Add to it half a pint of stock or water; stir a minute, and set back where it will keep warm, but not cook. Now take up the fillet, and skim all the fat off of the gravy; add water enough to make half a pint of gravy, also the sauce just made. Let this boil up, and add the juice of half a lemon, and more salt and pepper, if needed. Strain, and pour around the fillet. Garnish the dish with potato puffs and slices of lemon.

RoastHam.

Prepare the ham as for boiling, and if it is of good size (say ten pounds), boil three hours. Remove the skin, and put the ham in a baking pan. Let it cook two hours in a moderate oven. Serve with champagne sauce.

BROILING.

The fire for broiling must be clear, and for meats it must be hotter and brighter than for fish. Coals from hard wood or charcoal are best, but in all large towns and cities hard coal is nearly always used, except in hotels and restaurants, where there is usually a special place for broiling with charcoal. The double broiler is the very best thing in the market for broiling meats and fish. When the meat is placed in it, and the slide is slipped over the handles, all there is to do is to hold the broiler over the fire, or, if you have an open range, before the fire. A fork or knife need not go near the meat until it is on the dish. A great amount of the juice is saved. With the old-fashioned gridirons it is absolutely necessary to stick a fork into the meat to turn it, and although there are little grooves for the gravy to run into, what is saved in this way does not compare with what is actually kept within the meat where the double broiler is used. Professional cooks can turn a steak without running a fork into the meat, but not one in a hundred common cooks can do it.

MuttonChops.

Sprinkle the chops with salt, pepper and flour. Put them in the double broiler. Broil over or before the fire for eight minutes. Serve on a *hot* dish with butter, salt and pepper for tomato sauce. The fire for chops should not be as hot as for steak. Chops can be seasoned with salt and pepper, wrapped in buttered paper and broiled ten minutes over a hot fire.

BeefSteak.

Have it cut thick. It will never be good, rich and juicy if only from one-fourth to one-half an inch thick. It ought to be at least three-quarters of an inch thick. Trim off any suet that may be left on it, and dredge with salt, pepper and flour. Cook in the double broiler, over or before clear coals, for ten minutes, if to be rare, twelve, if to be rather well done. Turn the meat constantly. Serve on a hot dish with butter and salt, or with mushroom sauce, *maitre d' Hôtel* butter or tomato sauce. Do not stick a knife or fork into the meat to try it. This is the way many people spoil it. Pounding is another bad habit: much of the juice of the meat is lost. When, as it sometimes happens, there is no convenience for broiling, heat the frying pan very hot, then sprinkle with salt, and lay in the steak. Turn frequently.

MISCELLANEOUSMODES.

BraisedBeef.

Take six or eight pounds of the round or the face of the rump, and lard with quarter of a pound of salt pork. Put six slices of pork in the bottom of the braising pan, and as soon as it begins to fry, add two onions, half a small carrot and half a small turnip, all cut fine. Cook these until they begin to brown; then draw them to one side of the pan and put in the beef, which has been well dredged with salt, pepper and flour. Brown on all sides, and then add one quart of boiling water and a bouquet of sweet herbs; cover, and cook *slowly* in the oven for four hours, basting every twenty minutes. Take up, and finish the gravy as for braised tongue. Or, add to the gravy half a can of tomatoes, and cook for ten minutes. Strain, pour around the beef, and serve.

Fricandeau of Veal.

Have a piece of veal, weighing about eight pounds, cut from that part of the leg called the cushion. Wet the vegetable masher, and beat the veal smooth; then lard one side thickly. Put eight slices of pork in the bottom of the braising-pan; place the veal on this, larded side up. Add two small onions, half a small turnip, two slices of carrot, one clove and a bouquet of sweet herbs--these to be at the sides of the meat, not on top; and one quart of white stock or water. Dredge with salt, pepper and flour. Cover, and place in a rather moderate oven. Cook three hours, basting every fifteen minutes. If cooked rapidly the meat will be dry and stringy, but if slowly, it will be tender and juicy. When done, lift carefully from the pan. Melt four table-spoonfuls of glaze, and spread on the meat with a brush. Place in the open oven for five minutes. Add one cupful of hot water to the contents of the braising-pan. Skim off all the fat, and then add one heaping teaspoonful of corn-starch, which has been mixed with a little cold water. Let it boil one minute; then strain, and return to the fire. Add two table-spoonfuls of glaze, and when this is melted, pour the sauce around the fricandeau, and serve. Potato balls, boiled for twelve minutes in stock, and then slightly browned in the oven, make a pretty garnish for this dish. It is also served on a bed of finely-chopped spinach or mashed potatoes.

Leg of Lamb à la Française.

Put a leg of lamb, weighing about eight pounds, in as small a kettle as will hold it. Put in a muslin bag one onion, one small white turnip, a few green celery leaves, three sprigs each of sweet marjoram and summer savory, four cloves and twelve allspice. Tie the bag and place it in the kettle with the lamb; then pour on two quarts of boiling water. Let this come to a boil, and then skim carefully. Now add four heaping table-spoonfuls of flour, which has been mixed with one cupful of cold water, two table-spoonfuls of salt and a speck of cayenne. Cover tight, and set back where it will just simmer for four hours. In the meantime make a pint and a half of veal or mutton force-meat, which make into little balls and fry brown. Boil six eggs hard.

At the end of four hours take up the Iamb. Skim all the fat off of the gravy and take out the bag of seasoning. Now put the kettle where the contents will boil rapidly for ten minutes. Put three table-spoonfuls of butter in the frying-pan, and when hot, stir in two of flour; cook until a dark brown, but not burned, and stir into the gravy. Taste to see if seasoned enough. Have the whites and yolks of the hard-boiled eggs chopped separately. Pour the gravy over the lamb; then garnish with the chopped eggs, making a hill of the whites, and capping it with part of the yolks. Sprinkle the remainder of the yolks over the lamb. Place the meat balls in groups around the dish. Garnish with parsley, and serve.

BraisedBr eastofLamb.

With a sharp knife, remove the bones from a breast of lamb; then season it well with salt and pepper, and roll up and tie firmly with twine. Put two table-spoonfuls of butter in the braising-pan, and when melted, add one onion, one slice of carrot and one of turnip, all cut fine. Stir for five minutes, and then put in the lamb, with a thick dredging of flour. Cover, and set back, where it will not cook rapidly, for half an hour; then add one quart of stock or boiling water, and place in the oven, where it will cook *slowly*, for one hour. Baste often. Take up the meat, skim all the fat off of the gravy, and then put it where it will boil rapidly for five minutes. Take the string from the meat. Strain the gravy, and pour over the dish. Serve very hot. Or serve with tomato or Bechamel sauce. The bones should be put in the pan with the meat, to improve the gravy.

Beef Stew.

Two pounds of beef (the round, flank, or any cheap part; if there is bone in it, two and a half pounds will be required), one onion, two slices of carrot, two of turnip, two potatoes, three table-spoonfuls of flour, salt, pepper, and a generous quart of water. Cut all the fat from the meat, and put it in a stew-pan; fry gently for ten or fifteen minutes. In the meantime cut the meat in small pieces, and season well with salt and pepper, and then sprinkle over it two table-spoonfuls of flour. Cut the vegetables in very small pieces, and put in the pot with the fat. Fry them five minutes, stirring well, to prevent burning. Now put in the meat, and move it about in the pot until it begins to brown; then add the quart of boiling water. Cover; let it boil up once, skim, and set back, where it will just bubble, for two and a half hours. Add the potatoes, cut in thin slices, and one table-spoonful of flour, which mix smooth with half a cupful of cold water, pouring about one-third of the water on the flour at first, and adding the rest when perfectly smooth. Taste to see if the stew is seasoned enough, and if it is not, add more salt and pepper. Let the stew come to a boil again, and cook ten minutes; then add dumplings. Cover tightly, and boil rapidly ten minutes longer.

Mutton, lamb or veal can be cooked in this manner. When veal is used, fry out two slices of pork, as there will not be much fat on the meat. Lamb and mutton must have some of the fat put aside, as there is so much on these meats that they are otherwise very gross.

Irish Stew.

About two pounds of the neck of mutton, four onions, six large potatoes, salt, pepper, three pints of water and two table-spoonfuls of flour. Cut the mutton in handsome pieces. Put about half the fat in the stew-pan, with the onions, and stir for eight or ten minutes over a hot fire; then put in the meat, which sprinkle with the flour, salt and pepper. Stir ten minutes, and add the water, boiling. Set for one hour where it will simmer; then add the potatoes, peeled, and cut in quarters. Simmer an hour longer, and serve. You can cook dumplings with this dish, if you choose. They are a great addition to all kinds of stews and ragouts.

Toad in the Hole.

This is an English dish, and a good one, despite the unpleasant name. One pound of round steak, one pint of milk, one cupful of flour, one egg, and salt and pepper. Cut the steak into dice. Beat the egg very light; add milk to it, and then half a teaspoonful of salt. Pour upon the flour, gradually, beating very light and smooth. Butter a two-quart dish, and in it put the meat. Season well, and pour over it the batter. Bake an hour in a moderate oven. Serve hot. This dish can be made with mutton and lamb in place of steak.

Scotch Roll.

Remove the tough skin from about five pounds of the flank of beef. A portion of the meat will be found thicker than the rest. With a sharp knife, cut a thin layer from the thick part, and lay upon the thin. Mix together three table-spoonfuls of salt, one of sugar, half a teaspoonful of pepper, one-eighth of a teaspoonful of clove and one teaspoonful of summer savory. Sprinkle this over the meat, and then sprinkle with three table-spoonfuls of vinegar. Roll up, and tie with twine. Put away in a cold place for twelve hours When it has stood this time, place in a stew-pan, with boiling water to cover, and simmer gently for three hours and a half. Mix four heaping table-spoonfuls of flour with half a cupful of cold water, and stir into the gravy. Season to taste with salt and pepper. Simmer half an hour longer. This dish is good hot or cold.

POULTRY AND GAME.

To Clean and Truss Poultry.

First singe, by holding the bird over a blazing paper. It is best to do this over the open stove, when all the particles of burnt paper will fall into the fire. Next open the vent and draw out the internal organs, if this has not been done at the butcher's. Be careful not to break the gall bladder. Wash quickly in one water. If there are large black pin-feathers, take out what you can with the point of a knife, (it is impossible to get out all). Cut the oil bag from the tail. Be sure that you have taken out every part of the wind-pipe, the lights and crop. Turn the skin back, and cut the neck quite short. Fill the crop with dressing, and put some in the body also. With a short skewer, fasten the legs together at the joint where the feet were cut off. [Be careful, in cutting off the feet of game or poultry, to cut in the joint. If you cut above, the ligaments that hold the flesh and bones together will be severed, and in cooking, the meat will shrink, leaving a bare, unsightly bone. Besides, you will have nothing to hold the skewer, if the ligaments are cut off.] Run the skewer into the bone of the tail, and tie firmly with a long piece of twine. Now take a longer skewer, and run through the two wings, fastening them firmly to the sides of the bird. With another short skewer, fasten the skin of the neck on to the back-bone. Place the bird on its breast, and draw the strings, with which the legs were tied, around the skewers in the wings and neck; pass them across the back three times, and tie very tightly. By following these directions, you will have the bird in good shape, and all the strings on the back, so that you will avoid breaking the handsome crust that always forms on properly basted and roasted poultry. When cooked, first cut the strings, then draw out the skewers. The fat that comes from the vent and the gizzard of chickens, should be tried out immediately and put away for shortening and frying. That of geese, turkeys and ducks is of too strong a flavor to be nice in cookery.

To clean the giblets: Cut the gall-bag from the lobe of the liver, cutting a little of the liver with it, so as not to cut into the bag. Press the heart between the finger and thumb, to extract all the blood. With a sharp knife, cut lightly around the gizzard, and draw off the outer coat, leaving the lining coat whole. If you cannot do that (and it does require practice), cut in two, and after removing the filling, take out the lining. When the poultry is to be boiled, and is stuffed, the vent must be sewed with mending cotton or soft twine. Unless the bird is full of dressing, this will not be necessary in roasting.

Fowl and Pork.

Clean and truss, pin in the floured cloth and put into water in which one pound of rather lean pork has been boiling three hours. The time of cooking depends upon the age of the fowl. If they are not more than a year old an hour and a half will be enough, but if very old they may need three hours. The quantity of pork given is for only a pair of fowl, and more must be used if a large number of birds be cooked. Serve with egg sauce. The liquor should be saved for soups.

Boiled Fowl with Macaroni.

Break twelve sticks of macaroni in pieces about two inches long; throw them into one quart of boiling water, add a table-spoonful of salt and half a table-spoonful of pepper. Boil rapidly for twelve minutes; then take up, and drain off all the water. Season with one table-spoonful of butter and one teaspoonful of salt. After the fowl have been singed and cleaned, stuff with the macaroni. Truss them, and then pin in a floured cloth and plunge into enough boiling water to cover them. Boil rapidly for fifteen minutes; then set back where they will just simmer for from one and a half to two and a half hours. The time of cooking depends upon the age of the birds. Serve with an egg or Bechamel sauce. The quantity of macaroni given is for two fowl. Plain boiled macaroni should be served with this dish.

Boiled Turkey with Celery.

Chop half a head of celery very fine. Mix with it one quart of bread crumbs, two scant table-spoonfuls of salt, half a teaspoonful of pepper, two heaping table-spoonfuls of butter and two eggs. Stuff the turkey with this; sew up and truss. Wring a large square of white cotton cloth out of cold water, and dredge it thickly with flour. Pin the turkey in this, and plunge into boiling water. Let it boil rapidly for fifteen minutes; then set back where it will simmer. Allow three hours for a turkey weighing nine pounds, and twelve minutes for every additional pound. Serve with celery sauce. The stuffing may be made the same as above, only substitute oysters for celery, and serve with oyster sauce.

Boiled Turkey.

Clean and truss the same as for roasting. Rub into it two spoonfuls of salt, and put into boiling water to cover. Simmer gently three hours, if it weighs nine or ten pounds, and is tender. If old and tough it will take longer. Serve with oyster, celery or egg sauce. Pour some of the sauce over the turkey, and serve the rest in a gravy boat.

Roast Turkey.

Proceed the same with a turkey as with a chicken, allowing one hour and three-quarters for a turkey weighing eight pounds, and ten minutes for every additional pound.

Roast Turkey with Chestnut Stuffing and Sauce.

Clean the turkey, and lard the breast. Throw fifty large chestnuts into boiling water for a few minutes; then take them up, and rub off the thin, dark skin. Cover them with boiling water, and simmer for one hour; take them up, and mash fine. Chop one pound of veal and half a pound of salt pork very fine. Add half of the chestnuts to this, and add, also, half a teaspoonful of pepper, two table-spoonfuls of salt and one cupful of stock or water. Stuff the turkey with this. Truss, and roast as already directed. Serve with a chestnut sauce. The remaining half of the chestnuts are for this sauce.

Boned Turkey.

Get a turkey that has not been frozen (freezing makes it tear easily). See that every part is whole; one with a little break in the skin will not do. Cut off the legs, in the joints, and the tips of the wings. Do not draw the bird. Place it on its breast, and with a small, sharp boning knife, cut in a straight line through to the bone, from the neck down to that part of the bird where there is but little flesh, where it is all skin and fat. Begin at the neck, and run the knife between the flesh and the bones until you come to the wing.

Then cut the ligaments that hold the bones together and the tendons that hold the flesh to the bones. With the thumb and fore-finger, *press* the flesh from the smooth bone. When you come to the joint, carefully separate the ligaments and remove the bone. Do not try to take the bone from the next joint, as that is not in the way when carving, and it gives a more natural shape to the bird. Now begin at the wish-bone, and when that is free from the flesh, run the knife between the sides and the flesh, always using the fingers to press the meat from the smooth bones, as, for instance, the breast-bone and lower part of the sides. Work around the legs the same as you did around the wings, always using great care at the joints not to cut the skin. Drawing out the leg bones turns that part of the bird inside out. Turn the bird over, and proceed in the same manner with the other side. When all is detached, carefully draw the skin from the breast-bone; then run the knife between the fat and bone at the rump, leaving the small bone in the extreme end, as it holds the skewers. Carefully remove the flesh from the skeleton, and turn it right side out again. Rub into it two table-spoonfuls of salt and a little pepper, and fill with dressing. Sew up the back and neck and then the vent. Truss the same as if not boned. Take a strong piece of cotton cloth and pin the bird firmly in it, drawing very tight at the legs, as this is the broadest place, and the shape will not be good unless this precaution be taken. Steam three hours, and then place on a buttered tin sheet, which put in a baking pan. Baste well with butter, pepper, salt and flour. Roast one hour, basting every ten minutes, and twice with stock. When cold, remove the skewers and strings, and garnish with aspic jelly, cooked beets and parsley. To carve: First cut off the wings, then about two thick slices from the neck, where it will be quite fat, and then cut in thin slices. Serve jelly with each plate.

Filling for a turkey weighing eight pounds: The flesh of one chicken weighing four pounds, one pound of clear veal, half a pound of clear salt pork, one small capful of cracker crumbs, two eggs, one cupful of broth, two and a half table-spoonfuls of salt, half a teaspoonful of pepper, one teaspoonful of summer savory, one of sweet majoram, one of thyme, half a spoonful of sage, and, if you like, one table-spoonful of capers, one quart of oysters and two table-spoonfuls of onion juice. Have the meat uncooked and free from any tough pieces. Chop *very* fine. Add seasoning, crackers, etc., mix thoroughly, and use. If oysters are used, half a pound of the veal must be omitted. Where one cannot eat veal, use chicken instead. Veal is recommended for its cheapness. Why people choose boned turkey instead of a plain roast turkey or chicken, is not plain, for the flavor is not so good; but at the times and places where boned birds are used, it is a very appropriate dish. That is, at suppers, lunches and parties, where the guests are served standing, it is impracticable to provide anything that cannot be broken with a fork or spoon; therefore, the advantage of a boned turkey, chicken, or bird, is apparent. One turkey weighing eight pounds before being boned, will serve thirty persons at a party, if there are, also, say oysters, rolls, coffee, ices, cake and cream. If the supper is very elaborate the turkey will answer for one of the dishes for a hundred or more persons. If nothing more were gained in the boning of a bird, the knowledge of the anatomy and the help this will give in carving, pay to bone two or three chickens. It is advisable to bone at least two fowls before trying a turkey, for if you spoil them there is nothing lost, as they make a stew or soup.

Aspic jelly: One and a half pints of clear stock--beef if for amber jelly, and chicken or veal if for white; half a box of gelatine, the white of one egg, half a cupful of cold water, two cloves, one large slice of onion, twelve pepper-corns, one stalk of celery, salt. Soak gelatine two hours in the cold water. Then put on with other ingredients, the white of the egg being beaten with one spoonful of the cold stock. Let come to a boil, and set back where it will just simmer for twenty minutes. Strain through a napkin, turn into a mould or shallow dish, and put away to harden. The jelly can be made with the bones of the turkey and chicken, by washing them, covering with cold water and boiling down to about three pints; by then straining and setting away to cool, and in the morning skimming off all the fat and turning off the clear stock. The bones may, instead, be used for a soup.

Roast Goose.

Stuff the goose with a potato dressing made in the following manner: Six potatoes, boiled, pared and mashed fine and light; one table-spoonful of salt, one teaspoonful of pepper, one spoonful of sage, two table-spoonfuls of onion juice, two of butter. Truss, and dredge well with salt, pepper and flour. Roast before the fire (if weighing eight pounds) one hour and a half; in the oven, one hour and a quarter. Make gravy the same as for turkey. No butter is required for goose, it is so fat. Serve with apple sauce. Many people boil the goose half an hour before roasting, to take away the strong flavor. Why not have something else if you do not like the real flavor of the goose?

Roast Duck.

Ducks, to be good, must be cooked rare: for this reason it is best not to stuff. If, however, you do stuff them, use the goose dressing, and have it very hot. The better way is to cut an onion in two, and put into the body of the bird; then truss, and dredge with salt, pepper and flour, and roast, if before the fire, forty minutes, and if in the oven, thirty minutes. The fire must be very hot if the duck be roasted in the kitchen, and if in the oven, this must be a quick one. Serve with currant jelly and a sauce made the same as for turkey.

Roast Chicken.

Clean the chicken, and stuff the breast and part of the body with dressing made as follows: For a pair of chickens weighing between seven and eight pounds, take one quart of stale bread (being sure not to have any hard pieces), and break up in very fine crumbs. Add a table-spoonful of salt, a scant teaspoonful of pepper, a teaspoonful of chopped parsley, half a teaspoonful of powdered sage, one of summer savory and a scant half cupful of butter. Mix well together. This gives a rich dressing that will separate like rice when served. Now truss the chickens, and dredge well with salt. Take soft butter in the hand, and rub thickly over the chicken; then dredge rather thickly with flour. Place on the side, on the meat rack, and put into a hot oven for a few moments, that the flour in the bottom of the pan may brown. When it is browned, put in water enough to cover the pan. Baste every fifteen minutes with the gravy in the pan, and dredge with salt, pepper and flour. When one side is browned, turn, and brown the other. The last position in which the chicken should bake is on its back, that the breast may be nicely frothed and browned. The last basting is on the breast, and should be done with soft butter, and the breast should be dredged with flour. Putting the butter on the chicken at first, and then covering with flour, makes a paste, which keeps the juices in the chicken, and also supplies a certain amount of rich basting that is absorbed into the meat. It really does not take as much butter to baste poultry or game in this manner as by the old method of putting it on with a spoon after the bird began to cook. The water in the pan must often be renewed; and always be careful not to get in too much at a time. It will take an hour and a quarter to cook a pair of chickens, each weighing between three and a half and four pounds; anything larger, an hour and a half. A sure sign that they are done is the readiness of joints to separate from the body. If the chickens are roasted in the tin-kitchen, before the fire, it will take a quarter of an hour longer than in the oven.

Gravy for chickens: Wash the hearts, livers, gizzards and necks and put on to boil in three pints of water; boil down to one pint. Take them all up. Put the liver on a plate, and mash fine with the back of the spoon; return it to the water in which it was boiled. Mix two table-spoonfuls of flour with half a cupful of cold water. Stir into the gravy, season well with salt and pepper, and set back where it will simmer, for twenty minutes. Take up the chickens, and take the meat rack out of the pan. Then tip the pan to one side, to bring all the gravy together. Skim off the fat. Place the pan on top of the stove and turn into it one cupful of water. Let this boil up, in the meantime scraping everything from the sides and bottom of the pan. Turn this into the made gravy, and let it all boil together while you are removing the skewers and strings from the chickens.

Chicken à la Matelote.

Cut up an uncooked chicken. Rub in butter and flour, and brown in an oven. Fry in four table-spoonfuls of chicken fat or butter, for about twenty minutes, a small carrot, onion and parsnip, all cut into dice. When the chicken is browned, put it in a stew-pan with the cooked vegetables and one quart of white stock. Then into the fat in which the vegetables were fried, put two table-spoonfuls of flour, and cook until brown. Stir this in with the chicken. Add the liver, mashed fine, one table-spoonful of capers and salt and pepper to taste. Cook very gently three-quarters of an hour; then add one-fourth of a pound of mushrooms, cut in small pieces. Cook fifteen minutes longer. Serve with a border of boiled macaroni, mashed potatoes or rice.

Chicken à la Reine.

Clean, stuff and truss a pair of chickens, as for roasting. Dredge well with salt, pepper and flour. Cut a quarter of a pound of pork in slices, and put part on the bottom of a deep stew-pan with two slices of carrot and one large onion, cut fine. Stir over the fire until they begin to color; then put in the chickens, and lay the remainder of the pork over them. Place the stew-pan in a hot oven for twenty minutes; then add white stock to half cover the chicken (about two quarts), and a bouquet of sweet herbs. Dredge well with flour. Cover the pan and return to the oven. Baste about every fifteen minutes, and after cooking one hour, turn over the chickens. Cook, in all, two hours. Serve with Hollandaise sauce or with the sauce in which the chickens were cooked, it being strained over them.

Chicken à la Tartare.

Singe the chicken, and split down the back. Wipe thoroughly with a damp cloth. Dredge well with salt and pepper, cover thickly with softened butter, and dredge thickly on both sides with fine, dry bread crumbs. Place in a baking pan, the inside down, and cook in a very hot oven thirty minutes, taking care not to bum. Serve with Tartare sauce.

Broiled Chicken.

Singe the chicken, and split down the back, if not already prepared; and wipe with a damp cloth. Never wash it. Season well with salt and pepper. Take some soft butter in the right hand and rub over the bird, letting the greater part go on the breast and legs. Dredge with flour. Put in the double broiler, and broil over a moderate fire, having the breast turned to the heat at first. When the chicken is a nice brown, which will be in about fifteen minutes, place in a pan and put into a moderate oven for twelve minutes. Place on a hot dish, season, with salt, pepper and butter, and serve immediately. This rule is for a chicken weighing about two and a half pounds. The chicken is improved by serving with *maître d' hôtel* butter or Tartare sauce.

Chicken Stew with Dumplings.

One chicken or fowl, weighing about three pounds; one table-spoonful of butter, three of flour, one large onion, three slices of carrot, three of turnip, three pints of boiling water and salt and pepper. Cut the chicken in slices suitable for serving. Wash, and put in a deep stew-pan, add the water, and set on to boil. Put the carrot, turnip and onion, cut fine, in a sauce-pan, with the butter, and cook slowly half an hour, stirring often; then take up the vegetables in a strainer, place the strainer in the stew-pan with the chicken, and dip some of the water into it. Mash the vegetables with the back of a spoon, and rub as much as possible through the strainer. Now skim two spoonfuls of chicken fat from the water, and put in the pan in which the vegetables were cooked. When boiling hot, add the three table-spoonfuls of flour. Stir over the fire until a dark brown; then stir it in with the chicken, and simmer until tender. Season well with pepper and salt. The stew should only simmer all the while it is cooking. It must not boil hard. About two hours will be needed to cook a year old chicken. Twelve minutes before serving draw the stew-pan forward, and boil up; then put in the dumplings, and cook *ten* minutes. Take them up, and keep in the heater while you are dishing the chicken into the centre of the platter. Afterwards, place the dumplings around the edge. This is a very nice and economical dish, if pains are taken in preparing. One stewed chicken will go farther than two roasted.

Larded Grouse.

Clean and wash the grouse. Lard the breast and legs. Run a small skewer into the legs and through the tail. Tie firmly with twine. Dredge with salt, and rub the breast with soft butter; then dredge thickly with flour. Put into a quick oven. If to be very rare, cook twenty minutes; if wished better done, thirty minutes. The former time, as a general thing, suits gentlemen better, but thirty minutes is preferred by ladies. If the birds are cooked in a tin-kitchen, it should be for thirty or thirty-five minutes. When done, place on a hot dish, on which has been spread bread sauce. Sprinkle fried crumbs over both grouse and sauce. Garnish with parsley. The grouse may, instead, be served on a hot dish, with the parsley garnish, and the sauce and crumbs served in separate dishes. The first method is the better, however, as you get in the sauce all the gravy that comes from the birds.

Larded Partridges.

Partridges are cooked and served the same as grouse.

Larded Quail.

The directions for cooking and serving are the same as those for grouse, only that quails cook in fifteen minutes. All dry-meated birds are cooked in this way. The question is sometimes asked, Should ducks be larded? Larding is to give richness to a dry meat that does not have fat enough of its own; therefore, meats like goose, duck and mutton are *not* improved by larding.

Broiled Quail.

Split the quail down the back. Wipe with a damp towel. Season with salt and pepper, rub thickly with soft butter, and dredge with flour. Broil ten minutes over clear coals. Serve on hot buttered toast, garnishing with parsley.

Broiled Pigeons.

Prepare, cook and serve the same as quail They should be young for broiling, squabs being the best.

Broiled Small Birds.

All small birds can be broiled according to the directions for quail, remembering that for extremely small ones it takes a very bright fire. As the birds should be only browned, the time required is very brief.

Small Birds, Roasted.

Clean, by washing quickly in one water after they have been drawn. Season with salt and pepper. Cut slices of salt pork *very thin*, and with small skewers, fasten a slice around each bird. Run a long skewer through the necks of six or eight, and rest it on a shallow baking-pan. When all the birds are arranged, put into a *hot* oven for twelve minutes, or before a hot fire for a quarter of an hour. Serve on toast.

Potted Pigeons.

Clean and wash one dozen pigeons. Stand them on their necks in a deep earthen or porcelain pot, and turn on them a pint of vinegar. Cut three large onions in twelve pieces, and place a piece on each pigeon. Cover the pot, and let it stand all night In the morning take out the pigeons, and throw away the onions and vinegar. Fry, in a deep stew-pan, six slices of fat pork, and when browned, take them up, and in the fat put six onions, sliced fine. On these put the pigeons, having first trussed them, and dredge well with salt pepper and flour. Cover, and cook slowly for forty-five minutes, stirring occasionally; then add two quarts of boiling water, and simmer gently two hours. Mix four heaping table-spoonfuls of flour with a cupful of cold water, and stir in with the pigeons. Taste to see if there is enough seasoning, and if there is not, add more. Cook half an hour longer. Serve with a garnish of rice or riced potatoes. More or less onion can be used; and, if you like it so, spice the gravy slightly.

Pigeons in Jelly.

Wash and truss one dozen pigeons. Put them in a kettle with four pounds of the shank of veal, six cloves, twenty-five pepper-corns, an onion that has been fried in one spoonful of butter, one stalk of celery, a bouquet of sweet herbs and four and a half quarts of water. Have the veal shank broken in small pieces. As soon as the contents of the kettle come to a boil, skim carefully, and set for three hours where they will just simmer. After they have been cooking one hour, add two table-spoonfuls of salt. When the pigeons are done, take them up, being careful not to break them, and remove the strings. Draw the kettle forward, where it will boil rapidly, and keep there for forty minutes; then strain the liquor through a napkin, and taste to see if seasoned enough. The water should have boiled down to two and a half quarts. Have two moulds that will each hold six pigeons. Put a thin layer of the jelly in these, and set on ice to harden. When hard, arrange the pigeons in them, and cover with the jelly, which must be cold, but liquid. Place in the ice chest for six or, better still, twelve hours. There should be only one layer of the pigeons in the mould.

To serve: Dip the mould in a basin of warm water for one minute, and turn on a cold dish. Garnish with pickled beets and parsley. A Tartare sauce can be served with this dish.

If squabs are used, two hours will cook them. All small birds, as well as partridge, grouse, etc., can be prepared in the same manner. Remember that the birds must be cooked tender, and that the liquor must be so reduced that it will become jellied.

Roast Rabbit.

First make a stuffing of a pound of veal and a quarter of a pound of pork, simmered two hours in water to cover; four crackers, rolled fine; a table-spoonful of salt, a scant teaspoonful of pepper, a teaspoonful of summer savory, a large table-spoonful of butter and one and a quarter cupfuls of the broth in which the veal and pork were cooked. Chop the meat fine, add the other ingredients, and put on the fire to heat. Cut off the rabbit's head, open the vent, and draw. Wash clean, and season with salt and pepper. Stuff while the dressing is hot, and sew up the opening. Put the rabbit on its knees, and skewer in that position. Rub thickly with butter, dredge with flour, and put in the baking pan, the bottom of which should be covered with hot water. Bake half an hour in a quick oven, basting frequently. Serve with a border of mashed potatoes, and pour the gravy over the rabbit.

Curry of Rabbit.

Cut the rabbit in small pieces. Wash, and cook the same as chicken curry.

Saddle of Venison.

Carefully scrape off the hair, and wipe with a damp towel; Season well with salt and pepper, and roll up and skewer together. Rub thickly with soft butter and dredge thickly with flour. Roast for an hour before a clear fire or in a *hot* oven, basting frequently. When half done, if you choose, baste with a few spoonfuls of claret. Or, you can have one row of larding on each side of the back-bone. This gives a particularly nice flavor.

To make the gravy: Pour off all the fat from the baking pan, and put in the pan a cupful of boiling water. Stir from the sides and bottom, and set back where it will keep hot. In a small frying-pan put one table-spoonful of butter, a small slice of onion, six pepper-corns and four whole cloves. Cook until the onion is browned, and then add a generous teaspoonful of flour.

Stir until this is browned; then, gradually, add the gravy in the pan. Boil one minute. Strain, and add half a teaspoonful of lemon juice and three tablespoonfuls of currant jelly. Serve both venison and gravy very hot. The time given is for a saddle weighing between ten and twelve pounds. All the dishes and plates for serving must be hot. Venison is cooked in almost the same manner as beef, always remembering that it must be served *rare* and *hot*.

Roast Leg of Venison.

Draw the dry skin from the meat, and wipe with a damp towel. Make a paste with one quart of flour and a generous pint of cold water. Cover the venison with this, and place before a hot fire, if to be roasted in the tin kitchen, or else in a very hot oven. As the paste browns, baste it frequently with the gravy in the pan. When it has been cooking one hour and a half, take off the paste, cover with butter, and dredge thickly with flour. Cook one hour longer, basting frequently with butter, salt and flour. Make the gravy the same as for a saddle of venison, or serve with game sauce. The time given is for a leg weighing about fifteen pounds.

ENTREES.

Fillet of Beef, Larded.

The true fillet is the tenderloin, although sometimes one will see a rib roast, boned and rolled, called a fillet. A short fillet, weighing from two and a half to three pounds (the average weight from a very large rump), will suffice for ten persons at a dinner where this is served as one course; and if a larger quantity is wanted a great saving will still be made if two short fillets are used. They cost about two dollars, while a large one, weighing the same amount, would cost five dollars, Fillet of beef is one of the simplest, safest and most satisfactory dishes that a lady can prepare for either her own family or guests. After a single trial she will think no more of it than of broiling a beef steak. First, remove from the fillet, with a sharp knife, every shred of muscle, ligament and thin, tough skin. If it is not then of a good round shape, skewer it into shape. Draw a line through the centre, and lard with two rows of pork, having them meet at this line. Dredge well with salt, pepper and flour, and put, without water, in a very small pan. Place in a hot oven for thirty minutes. Let it be in the lower part of the oven the first ten minutes, then place on the upper grate. Serve with mushroom, Hollandaise or tomato sauce, or with potato balls. If with sauce, this should be poured around the fillet, the time given cooks a fillet of any size, the shape being such that it will take half an hour for either two or six pounds. Save the fat trimmed from the fillet for frying, and the lean part for soup stock.

Fillet of Beef à la Hollandaise.

Trim and cut the short fillet into slices about half an inch thick. Season these well with salt, and then lay in a pan with six table-spoonfuls of butter, just warm enough to be oily. Squeeze the juice of a quarter of a lemon over them. Let them stand one hour; then dip lightly in flour, place in the double broiler, and cook for six minutes over a very bright fire. Have a mound of mashed potatoes in the centre of a hot dish, and rest the slices against this. Pour a Hollandaise sauce around. Garnish with parsley.

Fillet of Beef à l'Allemand.

Trim the fillet and skewer it into a good shape. Season well with pepper and salt. Have one egg and half a teaspoonful of sugar well beaten together; roll the fillet in this and then in bread crumbs. Bake in the oven for thirty minutes. Serve with Allemand sauce poured around it.

Fillet of Beef in Jelly.

Trim a short fillet, and cut a deep incision in the side, being careful not to go through to the other side or the ends. Fill this with one cupful of veal, prepared as for quenelles, and the whites of three hard-boiled eggs, cut into rings. Sew up the openings, and bind the fillet into good shape with broad bands of cotton cloth. Put in a deep stew-pan two slices of ham and two of pork, and place the fillet on them; then put in two calf's feet, two stalks of celery and two quarts of clear stock. Simmer gently two hours and a half. Take up the fillet, and set away to cool. Strain the stock, and set away to harden. When hard, scrape of every particle of fat, and put on the fire in a clean sauce-pan, with half a slice of onion and the whites of two eggs, beaten with four table-spoonfuls of cold water. When this boils, season well with salt, and set back where it will just simmer for half an hour; then strain through a napkin. Pour a little of the jelly into a two-quart charlotte russe mould (half an inch deep), and set on the ice to harden. As soon as it is hard, decorate with the egg rings. Add about three spoonfuls of the liquid jelly, to set the eggs. When hard, add enough jelly to cover the eggs, and when this is also hard, trim the ends of the fillet, and draw out the thread. Place in the centre of the mould, and cover with the remainder of the jelly. If the fillet floats, place a slight weight on it. Set in the ice chest to harden. When ready to serve, place the mould in a pan of warm water for half a minute, and then turn out the fillet gently upon a dish. Garnish with a circle of egg rings, each of which has a stoned olive in the centre. Put here and there a sprig of parsley.

Alamode Beef.

Six pounds of the upper part, or of the vein, of the round of beef, half a pound of fat salt pork, three table-spoonfuls of butter, two onions, half a carrot, half a turnip, two table-spoonfuls of vinegar, one of lemon juice, one heaping table-spoonful of salt, half a teaspoonful of pepper, two cloves, six allspice, a small piece of stick cinnamon, a bouquet of sweet herbs, two scant quarts of boiling water and four table-spoonfuls of flour. Cut the pork in thick strips--as long as the meat is thick, and, with a large larding needle (which comes for this purpose), draw these through the meat. If you do not have the large needle, make the holes with the boning knife or the carving steel, and press the pork through with the fingers. Put the butter in a six-quart stew-pan, and when it melts, add the vegetables, cut fine. Let them cook five minutes, stirring all the while. Put in the meat, which has been well dredged with the flour; brown on one aide, and then turn, and brown the other. Add one quart of the water; stir well, and then add the other, with the spice, herbs, vinegar, salt and pepper. Cover tightly, and *simmer gently* four hours. Add the lemon juice. Taste the gravy, and, if necessary, add more salt and pepper. Let it cook twenty minutes longer. Take up the meat, and draw the stew-pan forward, where it will boil rapidly, for ten or fifteen minutes, having first skimmed off all the fat. Strain the gravy on the beef, and serve. This dish may be garnished with, potato balls or button onions.

Macaronied Beef.

Six pounds of beef from the upper part of the round or the vein, a quarter of a pound of macaroni (twelve sticks), half a cupful of butter, four large onions, one quart of peeled and sliced tomatoes, or a quart can of the vegetable; two heaping table-spoonfuls of flour, salt, pepper and two cloves. Make holes in the beef with the large larding needle or the steel, and press the macaroni into them. Season with salt and pepper. Put the butter and the onions, which have been peeled and cut fine, in a six-quart stew-pan, and stir over the fire until a golden brown; then put in the meat, first drawing the onions aside. Dredge with the flour, and spread the top of the meat with the fried onions. Put in the spice and one quart of boiling water. Cover tightly, and simmer *slowly* for three hours; then add the tomato, and cook one hour longer. Take up the meat, and strain the gravy over it. Serve hot. The tomato may be omitted if one pint more of water and an extra table-spoonful of flour are used instead. Always serve macaroni with this dish.

Cannelon of Beef.

One thin slice of the upper part of the round of beef. Cut off all the fat, and so trim as to give the piece a regular shape. Put the trimmings in the chopping tray, with a quarter of a pound of boiled salt pork and one pound of lean cooked ham. Chop very fine; then add a speck of cayenne, one teaspoonful of mixed mustard, one of onion juice, one table-spoonful of lemon juice and three eggs. Season the beef with salt and pepper. Spread the mixture over it, and roll up. Tie with twine, being careful not to draw too tightly. Have six slices of fat pork fried in the braising pan. Cut two onions, two slices of carrot, and two of turnip into this, and stir for two minutes over the fire. Roll the cannelon in a plate of flour, and put it in the braising pan with the pork and vegetables. Brown slightly on all sides; then add one quart of boiling water, and place in the oven. Cook three hours, basting every fifteen minutes. When it has been cooking two hours, add half a cupful of canned tomatoes or two fresh ones. Taste to see if the gravy is seasoned enough; if it is not, add seasoning. The constant dredging with flour will thicken the gravy sufficiently. Slide the cake turner under the beef, and lift carefully on to a hot dish. Cut the string in three or four places with a *sharp* knife, and gently draw it away from the meat. Skim off all the fat. Strain the gravy through a fine sieve on to the meat. Garnish with a border of toast or riced potatoes. Cut in thin slices with a sharp knife.

Cannelon of Beef, No. 2.

Two pounds of the round of beef, the rind of half a lemon, three sprigs of parsley, one teaspoonful of salt, barely one-fourth of a teaspoonful of pepper, a quarter of a nutmeg, two table-spoonfuls of melted butter, one raw egg and half a teaspoonful of onion juice. Chop meat, parsley and lemon rind very fine. Add other ingredients, and mix thoroughly. Shape, into a roll, about three inches in diameter and six in length. Roll in buttered paper, and bake thirty minutes, basting with butter and water. When cooked, place on a hot dish, gently unroll from the paper, and serve with Flemish sauce poured over it. You may serve tomato or mushroom sauce if you prefer either.

Beef Roulette.

Have two pounds of the upper part of the round, cut very thin. Mix together one cupful of finely-chopped ham, two eggs, one teaspoonful of mixed mustard, a speck of cayenne and three table-spoonfuls of stock or water. Spread upon the beef, which roll up firmly and tie with soft twine, being careful not to draw too tightly, for that would cut the meat as soon as it began to cook. Cover the roll with flour, and fry brown in four table-spoonfuls of ham or pork fat. Put it in as small a sauce-pan as will hold it. Into the fat remaining in the pan put two finely-chopped onions, and cook until a pale yellow; then add two table-spoonfuls of flour, and stir three minutes longer. Pour upon this one pint and a half of boiling water. Boil up once, and pour over the roulette; then add two cloves, one-fourth of a teaspoonful of pepper and one heaping teaspoonful of salt. Cover the sauce-pan, and set where it will simmer slowly for three hours. After the first hour and a half, turn the roulette over. Serve hot; with the gravy strained over it. It is also nice to serve cold for lunch or supper. Ham force-meat balls and parsley make a pretty garnish.

Beef Olives.

One and a half pounds of beef, cut very thin. Trim off the edges and fat; then cut in strips three inches wide and four long; season well with salt and pepper. Chop fine the trimmings and the fat Add three table-spoonfuls of powdered cracker, one teaspoonful of sage and savory, mixed, one-fourth of a teaspoonful of pepper and two teaspoonfuls of salt. Mix very thoroughly and spread on the strips of beef. Roll them up, and tie with twine. When all are done, roll in flour. Fry brown a quarter of a pound of pork. Take it out of the pan, and put the olives in. Fry brown, and put in a small sauce-pan that can be tightly covered. In the fat remaining in the pan put one table-spoonful of flour, and stir until perfectly smooth and brown; then pour in, gradually, nearly a pint and a half of boiling water. Stir for two or three minutes, season to taste with salt and pepper, and pour over the olives. Cover the sauce-pan, and let simmer two hours. Take up at the end of this time and cut the strings with a sharp knife. Place the olives in a row on a dish, and pour the gravy over them.

Veal Olives.

These are made in the same manner, except that a dressing, like chicken dressing, is made for them. For one and a half pounds of veal take three crackers, half a table-spoonful of butter, half a teaspoonful of savory, one-fourth of a teaspoonful of sage, a teaspoonful of salt, a very little pepper and an eighth of a cupful of water. Spread the strips with this, and proceed as for beef olives.

Fricandelles of Veal.

Two pounds of clear veal, half a cupful of finely-chopped cooked ham, one cupful of milk, one cupful of bread crumbs, the juice of half a lemon, one table-spoonful of salt, half a teaspoonful of pepper, one cupful of butter, a pint and a half of stock, three table-spoonfuls of flour. Chop the veal fine. Cook the bread crumbs and milk until a smooth paste, being careful not to burn. Add to the chopped veal and ham, and when well mixed, add the seasoning and four table-spoonfuls of the butter. Mix thoroughly, and form into balls about the size of an egg. Have the yolks of three eggs well beaten, and use to cover the balls. Fry these, till a light brown, in the remainder of the butter, being *very* careful not to burn. Stir the three table-spoonfuls of flour into the butter that remains after the balls are fried. Stir until dark brown, and then gradually stir the stock into it. Boil for two minutes. Taste to see if seasoned enough; then add the balls, and cook *very slowly* for one hour. Serve with a garnish of toast and lemon.

Fricandelles can be made with chicken, mutton, lamb and beef, the only change in the above directions being to omit the ham.

Braised Tongue.

Wash a fresh beef tongue, and, with a trussing needle, run a strong twine through the roots and end of it, drawing tightly enough to have the end meet the roots; then tie firmly. Cover with boiling water, and boil gently for two hours; then take up and drain. Put six table-spoonfuls of butter in the braising pan, and when hot, put in half a small carrot, half a small turnip and two onions, all cut fine. Cook five minutes, stirring all the time, and then draw to one side. Roll the tongue in flour, and put in the pan. As soon as browned on one side, turn, and brown the other. Add one quart of the water in which it was boiled, a bouquet of sweet herbs, one clove, a small piece of cinnamon and salt and pepper. Cover, and cook two hours in a slow oven, basting often with the gravy in the pan, and salt, pepper and flour. When it has been cooking an hour and a half, add the juice of half a lemon to the gravy. When done, take up. Melt two table-spoonfuls of glaze, and pour over the tongue. Place in the heater until the gravy is made. Mix one table-spoonful of corn-starch with a little cold water, and stir into the boiling gravy, of which there should be one pint. Boil one minute; then strain, and pour around the tongue. Garnish with parsley, and serve.

Fillets of Tongue.

Cut cold boiled tongue in pieces about four inches long, two wide and half an inch thick. Dip in melted butter and in flour. For eight fillets put two table-spoonfuls of butter in the frying-pan, and when hot, put in the tongue. Brown on both sides, being careful not to burn. Take up, and put one more spoonful of butter in the pan, and then one heaping teaspoonful of flour. Stir until dark brown; then add one cupful of stock, half a teaspoonful of parsley and one table-spoonful of lemon juice, or one tea-spoonful of vinegar. Let this boil up once, and then pour it around the tongue, which has been dished on thin strips of toast. Garnish with parsley, and serve. For a change, a table-spoonful of chopped pickles, or of capers, can be stirred into the sauce the last moment.

Escaloped Tongue.

Chop some cold tongue--not too fine, and have for each pint one table-spoonful of onion juice, one teaspoonful of chopped parsley, one heaping teaspoonful of salt, one teaspoonful of capers, one cupful of bread crumbs, half a cupful of stock and three table-spoonfuls of butter. Butter the escalop dish, and cover the bottom with bread crumbs. Put in the tongue, which has been mixed with the parsley, salt, pepper and capers, and add the stock, in which has been mixed the onion juice. Put part of the butter on the dish with the remainder of the bread crumbs, and then bits of butter here and there. Bake twenty minutes, and serve hot.

Tongue in Jelly.

Boil and skin either a fresh or salt tongue. When cold, trim off the roots. Have one and a fourth quarts of aspic jelly in the liquid state. Cover the bottom of a two-quart mould about an inch deep with it, and let it harden. With a fancy vegetable cutter, cut out leaves from cooked beets, and garnish the bottom of the mould with them. Gently pour in three table-spoonfuls of jelly, to set the vegetables. When this is hard, add jelly enough to cover the vegetables, and let the whole get very hard. Then put in the tongue, and about half a cupful of jelly, which should be allowed to harden, and so keep the meat in place when the remainder is added. Pour in the remainder of the jelly and set away to harden. To serve: Dip the mould for a few moments in a pan of warm water, and then gently turn on to a dish. Garnish with pickles and parsley. Pickled beet is especially nice.

Lambs' Tongues in Jelly.

Lambs' tongues are prepared the same as beef tongues. Three of four moulds, each holding a little less than a pint, will make enough for a small company, one tongue being put in each mould. The tongues can all be put on the same dish, or on two, if the table is long.

Lambs' Tongues, Stewed.

Six tongues, three heaping table-spoonfuls of butter, one large onion, two slices of carrot, three slices of white turnip, three table-spoonfuls of flour, one of salt, a little pepper, one quart of stock or water and a bouquet of sweet herbs. Boil the tongues one hour and a half in clear water; then take up, cover with cold water, and draw off the skins. Put the butter, onion, turnip and carrot in the stew-pan, and cook slowly for fifteen minutes; then add the flour, and cook until brown, stirring all the while. Stir the stock into this, and when it boils up, add the tongue, salt, pepper and herbs. Simmer gently for two hours. Cut the carrots, turnips and potatoes into cubes. Boil the potatoes in salted water ten minutes, and the carrots and turnips one hour. Place the tongues in the centre of a hot dish. Arrange the vegetables around them, strain the gravy, and pour over all. Garnish with parsley, and serve.

Stewed Ox Tails.

Two ox tails, three table-spoonfuls of butter, two of flour, one large onion, half a small carrot, three slices of turnip, two stalks of celery, two cloves, a pint and a half of stock or water, salt and pepper to taste. Divide the tails in pieces about four inches long. Cut the vegetables in small pieces. Let the butter get hot in the stew-pan; then add the vegetables, and when they begin to brown, add the flour. Stir for two minutes. Put in the tails, and add the seasoning and stock. Simmer gently three hours. Serve on a hot dish with gravy strained over them.

Ox Tails à la Tartare.

Three ox tails, two eggs, one cupful of bread crumbs, salt, pepper, one quart of stock, a bouquet of sweet herbs. Cut the tails in four-inch pieces, and put them on to boil with the stock and sweet herbs. Let them simmer two hours. Take up, drain and cool. When cold, dip them in the beaten eggs and in bread crumbs. Fry in boiling fat till a golden brown. Have Tartare sauce spread on the centre of a cold dish, and arrange the ox tails on this. Garnish with parsley, and serve.

Haricot of Ox Tails.

Three ox tails, two carrots, two onions, two small white turnips, three potatoes, three table-spoonfuls of butter, two of flour, three pints of water and salt and pepper to taste. Cut the tails in pieces about four inches long. Cut the onions very fine, and the carrots, turnips and potatoes into large cubes. Put the butter, meat and onion in the stew-pan and fry, stirring all the time, until the onions are a golden brown; then add the flour, and stir two minutes longer. Add the water, and when it comes to a boil, skim carefully. Set back where it will simmer. When it has been cooking one hour, add the carrots and turnips. Cook another hour, and then add the salt, pepper and potatoes. Simmer twenty minutes longer. Heap the vegetables in the centre of a hot dish, and arrange the tails around them. Pour the gravy over all, and serve.

Ragout of Mutton.

Three pounds of any of the cheap parts of mutton, six table-spoonfuls of butter, three of flour, twelve button onions, or one of the common size; one large white turnip, cut into little cubes; salt, pepper, one quart of water and a bouquet of sweet herbs. Cut the meat in small pieces. Put three table-spoonfuls each of butter and flour in the stew-pan, and when hot and smooth, add the meat. Stir until a rich brown, and then add water, and set where it will simmer. Put three table-spoonfuls of butter in a frying-pan, and when hot, put in the turnips and onions with a teaspoonful of flour. Stir all the time until a golden brown; then drain, and put with the meat. Simmer for an hour and a half. Garnish with rice, toasted bread, plain boiled macaroni or mashed potatoes. Small cubes of potato can be added half an hour before dishing. Serve very hot.

Ragout of Veal.

Prepare the same as mutton, using one table-spoonful more of butter, and cooking an hour longer.

Chicken Pie.

One fowl weighing between four and five pounds, half the rule for chopped paste (see chopped paste), three pints of water, one-fourth of a teaspoonful of pepper, one table-spoonful of salt (these last two quantities may be increased if you like), three table-spoonfuls of flour, three of butter, two eggs, one table-spoonful of onion juice and a bouquet of sweet herbs. Clean the fowl, and cut in pieces as for serving. Put it in a stew-pan with the hot water, salt, pepper and herbs. When it comes to a boil, skim, and set back where it will simmer one hour and a half. Take up the chicken, and place in a deep earthen pie dish. Draw the stew-pan forward where it will boil rapidly for fifteen minutes. Skim off the fat and take out the bouquet. Put the butter in a frying-pan, and when hot, add the flour. Stir until smooth, but not brown, and stir in the water in which the chicken was boiled. Cook ten minutes. Beat the eggs with one spoonful of cold water, and gradually add the gravy to them. Turn this into the pie dish. Lift the chicken with a spoon, that the gravy may fall to the bottom. Set away to cool. When cold, roll out a covering of paste a little larger than the top of the dish and about one-fourth of an inch thick. Cover the pie with this, having the edges turned into the dish. Roll the remainder of the paste the same as before, and with a thimble, or something as small, cut out little pieces all over the cover. Put this perforated paste over the first cover, turning out the edges and rolling slightly. Bake one hour in a moderate oven.

Pasties of Game and Poultry.

Make three pints of force-meat. (See force-meat for game.) Cut all the solid meat from four grouse. Lard each piece with very fine strips of pork. Put half a cupful of butter and a finely-cut onion in a frying-pan. Stir until the onion is yellow; then put in the grouse, and cook slowly, with the cover on, for forty minutes. Stir occasionally. Take up the grouse, and put three table-spoonfuls of flour with the butter remaining in the pan. Stir until brown; add one quart of stock, two table-spoonfuls of glaze, a bouquet of sweet herbs, and four cloves. Simmer twenty minutes, and strain. Butter a four-quart earthen dish, and cover the bottom and sides with the force-meat. Put in a layer of the grouse, and moisten well with the gravy, which must be highly seasoned with salt and pepper; then put in the yolks of six hard-boiled eggs, and the whites, cut into rings. Moisten with gravy, and add another layer of grouse, and of eggs and gravy. Twelve eggs should be used. Make a paste as for chicken pie. Cover with this, and bake one hour and a half. Serve either hot or cold.

Any kind of meat pasties can be made in the same manner. With a veal pastie put in a few slices of cooked ham.

Cold Game Pie.

Make three pints of force-meat. (See force-meat for game.) Cut all the meat from two partridges or grouse, and put the bones on to boil with three quarts of water and three pounds of a shank of veal. Fry four large slices of fat salt pork, and as soon as brown, take up, and into the fat put one onion, cut in slices. When this begins to turn yellow, take up, and put the meat of the birds in the pan. Dredge well with salt, pepper and flour, and stir constantly for four minutes; then take up, and put away to cool. Make a crust as directed for raised pies. Butter the French pie mould very thoroughly, and line with paste. Spread upon the paste--both upon the sides and bottom of the mould--a thin layer of fat salt pork, then a layer of force-meat, one of grouse, again one of force-meat, and so on until the pie is filled. Leave a space of about half an inch at the edge of the mould, and heap the filling in the centre. Moisten with half a cupful of well-seasoned stock. Roll the remainder of the paste into the shape of the top of the mould. Wet the paste at the edge of the mould with beaten egg; then put on the top, and press the top and side parts together. Cut a small piece of paste from the centre of the top crust, add a little more paste to it, and roll a little larger than the opening, which it is to cover. Cut the edges with the jagging iron, and, with the other end of the iron, stamp leaves or flowers. Place on the top of the pie. Bake in a slow oven three hours and a half. While the pie is baking the sauce can be prepared. When the bones and veal have been cooking two hours, add two cloves, a bouquet of sweet herbs and the fried onions. Cook one hour longer; then salt and pepper well, and strain. The water should be reduced in boiling to one quart. When the pie is baked, take the centre piece from the cover, and slightly press the tunnel into the opening. Pour slowly one pint of the hot gravy through this. Put back the cover, and set away to cool. The remainder of the gravy must be turned into a flat dish and put in a cold place to harden. When the pie is served, place the mould in the oven, or steamer, for about five minutes; then draw out the wires and open it. Slip the pie on to a cold dish, and garnish with the jellied gravy and parsley. This is nice for suppers or lunches. All kinds of game and meat can be prepared in the same manner.

Pâté de Foies Gras.

Make a paste with one quart of flour, as for raised pies, and put away in a cool place. Put four fat goose livers in a pint of sweet milk for two or three hours, to whiten them. Chop *very fine* two pounds of fresh pork, cut from the loin (it must not be too fat), and one pound of clear veal. Put one and a half cupfuls of milk on to boil with a blade of mace, an onion, two cloves, a small piece of nutmeg and a bouquet of sweet herbs. Cook all these for ten minutes; then strain the milk upon four table-spoonfuls of butter and two of flour, which have been well mixed. Add to this the chopped pork and veal and one of the livers, chopped fine; stir over the fire for ten minutes, being careful not to brown. Season well with pepper and salt, add four well-beaten eggs, and stir half a minute longer; then put away to cool. Cut half a pound of salt pork in slices as thin as shavings. Butter a French pie mould, holding about three quarts. Form three-fourths of the paste into a ball. Sprinkle the board with flour, and roll the paste out until about one-fourth of an inch thick. Take it up by the four corners and place it in the mould. Be very careful not to break it. With the hand, press the paste on the sides and bottom. The crust must come to the top of the mould. Put a layer of the pork shavings on the sides and bottom, then a thick layer of the force-meat. Split the livers, and put half of them in; over them sprinkle one table-spoonful of onion juice, salt, pepper, and, if you like, a table-spoonful of capers. Another layer of force-meat, again the liver and seasoning, and then the force-meat. On this last layer put salt pork shavings. Into the remaining paste roll three table-spoonfuls of washed butter, and roll the paste, as nearly as possible, into the shape of the top of the pie mould. Cut a small piece from the centre. The filling of the pie should have been heaped a little toward the centre, leaving a space of about one inch and a half at the edges. Brush with beaten egg the paste that is in this space. Put on the top crust, and, with the fore-finger and thumb, press the two crusts together. Roll the piece of paste cut from the centre of the cover a little larger, and cover the opening with it. From some puff-paste trimmings, cut out leaves, and decorate the cover with them. Place in a moderate oven, and bake slowly two hours. Have a pint and a half of hot veal stock (which will become jellied when cold) well seasoned with pepper, salt, whole spice and onion. When the *pâté* is taken from the oven, take off the small piece that was put on the centre of the cover. Insert a tunnel in the opening and pour the hot stock through it. Replace the cover, and set away to cool. When the *pâté* is to be served, place it in the oven for about five minutes, that it may slip from the mould easily. Draw out the wires which fasten the sides of the mould, and slide the *pâté* upon the platter. Garnish the dish with parsley and small strips of cucumber pickles.

Truffles and mushrooms can be cut up and put in the *pâté* in layers, the same as the liver and at the same time. The Strasburg fat livers (*foies gras*) come in little stone pots, and cost from a dollar to two dollars per pot.

Chartreuse of Chicken.

Make the force-meat as for *quenelles* of chicken. Simmer two large chickens in white stock for half an hour. Take up, and let cool. Have a pickled tongue boiled tender. Cut thin slices from the breast of the chickens, and cut these in squares. Cut the tongue in slices, and these in turn in squares the same size as the chicken. Butter a four-quart mould, and arrange the chicken and tongue handsomely on the bottom and sides, being careful to have the pieces fit closely together. Have note paper cut to fit the bottom and sides. Butter it well, and cover about an inch deep with the force-meat. Take up the bottom piece by the four corners and fit it into the mould, the meat side down. Pour a little hot water into any kind of a flat-bottomed tin basin, and put this in the mould and move it over the papers, to melt the butter; then lift out the paper. Place the papers on the side in the same way as on the bottom and melt the butter by rolling a bottle of hot water over them. Remove these papers, and set the mould in a cold place until the filling is ready. Cut from the tenderest part of the chicken enough meat to make two quarts. Cut four large, or six small, mushrooms and four truffles in strips. Put half a cupful of butter, half a large onion, four cloves, a blade of mace, a slice of carrot, one of turnip and a stalk of celery in a sauce-pan, and cook five minutes, stirring all the while; then add five table-spoonfuls of flour. Stir until it begins to brown, when add one quart of the stock in which the chickens were cooked, a bouquet of sweet herbs, and salt and pepper. Simmer twenty minutes; strain, and add to the chicken. Return to the fire, and simmer twenty minutes longer, and set away to cool. When cold, put a layer of the chicken in the mould, and a light layer of the truffles and mushrooms. Continue this until the form is nearly full, and then cover with the remainder of the force-meat. Spread buttered paper upon it, and put in a cool place until cooking time, when steam two hours. Turn carefully upon the dish. Brush over with three table-spoonfuls of melted glaze. Pour one pint of supreme sauce around it, and serve.

The force-meat must be spread evenly on the paper and smoothed with a knife that has been dipped in hot water. All kinds of meat *chartreuses* can be made in this manner.

Chartreuse of Vegetables and Game.

Six large carrots, six white turnips, two large heads of cabbage, two onions, two quarts of stock, three grouse, one pint of brown sauce, four table-spoonfuls of glaze, two cloves, a bouquet of sweet herbs, one pound of mixed salt pork and one cupful of butter. Scrape and wash the carrots, and peel and wash the turnips. Boil for twenty minutes in salted water. Pour off the water, and add three pints of stock and a teaspoonful of sugar. Simmer gently one hour. Take up, drain, and set away to cool. Cut the cabbage in four parts. Wash, and boil twenty minutes in salted water. Drain in the colander, and return to the fire with a pint of stock, the cloves, herbs and onions, tied in a piece of muslin; a quarter of a cupful of butter and the pork and grouse. Cover the sauce-pan, and place where the contents will just simmer for two hours and a half. When cooked, put the grouse and pork on a dish to cool. Turn the cabbage into the colander, first taking out the spice and onion. Press all the juice from the cabbage and chop very fine. Season with salt and pepper, and put away to cool. Butter a plain mould holding about four quarts. Butter note paper, cut to fit the sides and bottom, and line the mould with it. Cut the cold turnips and carrots in thick slices, and then in pieces all the same size and shape, but of any design you wish. Line the sides and bottom of the mould with these, being particular to have the pieces come together. Have the yellow and white arranged in either squares or rows. With the chopped cabbage put half a pint of the brown sauce and two spoonfuls of the glaze. Stir over the fire for six minutes. Spread a thick layer of this on the vegetables, being careful not to displace them. Cut each grouse into six pieces. Season with salt and pepper, and pack closely in the mould. Moisten with the remaining half pint of brown sauce. Cover with the remainder of the cabbage. Two hours before serving time, place in a steamer and cook. While the *chartreuse* is steaming, make the sauce. Put two table-spoonfuls of butter in a stew-pan, and when hot, add two table-spoonfuls of flour. Stir until a dark brown; then add the stock in which the cabbage was cooked and enough of that in which the turnips and carrots were cooked to make a quart. Stir until it boils; add two spoonfuls of glaze, and set back where it will just simmer for one hour. Skim off the fat, and strain. When the *chartreuse* is done, take up and turn gently upon the dish. Lift the mould *very* carefully. Take off the paper. Pour two table-spoonfuls of the sauce on the *chartreuse* and the remainder around it. The vegetable *chartreuse* can be made with any kind of game or meat.

Chartreuse of Chicken and Macaroni.

One large fowl, about four and a half or five pounds, boiled tender; half a box of gelatine, one cupful of broth in which the chicken was boiled, one cupful of cream, salt, pepper, fourteen ounces of macaroni. Just cover the fowl with boiling water, and simmer until very tender, the time depending upon the age, but being from one to two hours if the bird is not more than a year old. Take off all the skin and fat, and cut the meat in thin, delicate pieces. Soak the gelatine two hours in half a cupful of cold water, and dissolve it in the cupful of boiling broth; add to the cream, and season highly. Have the chicken well seasoned, also. Put the macaroni in a large flat pan with boiling water to cover, and boil rapidly for three minutes. Drain off the water, and place the macaroni on a board, having about twelve pieces in a bunch. Cut in pieces about three-fourths of an inch long. Butter a two-quart mould (an oval charlotte russe mould is the best) very thickly, and stick the macaroni closely over the bottom and sides. When done, put the chicken in lightly and evenly, and add the sauce very gradually. Steam one hour. Serve either cold or hot. Great care must be taken in dishing. Place the platter over the mould and turn platter and mould simultaneously. Let the dish rest a minute, and then gently remove the mould. Serve immediately. A long time is needed to line the mould with the macaroni, but this is such a handsome, savory dish as to pay to have it occasionally. If you prefer, you can use all broth, and omit the cream.

Galatine of Turkey.

Bone the turkey, and push the wings and legs inside of the body. Make three pints of ham force-meat. Cut a cold boiled tongue in thin slices. Season the turkey with salt and pepper, and spread on a board, inside up. Spread a layer of the force-meat on this, and then a layer of tongue. Continue this until all the tongue and force-meat are used. Roll the bird into a round form, and sew up with mending cotton. Wrap tightly in a strong piece of cotton cloth, which must be either pinned or sewed to keep it in position. Put in a porcelain kettle the bones of the turkey, two calf's feet, four pounds of the knuckle of veal, an onion, two slices of turnip, two of carrot, twenty peppercorns, four cloves, two stalks of celery, one table-spoonful of salt and three quarts of water. When this comes to a boil, skim, and put the turkey in. Set back where it will just simmer for three hours. Take up and remove the wrapping, put on a clean piece of cloth that has been wet in cold water, and place in a dish. Put three bricks in a flat baking pan, and place on top of the bird. Set away in a cool place over night. In the morning take off the weights and cloth. Place on a dish, the smooth side up. Melt four table-spoonfuls of glaze, and brush the turkey with it. Garnish with the jelly, and serve. Or, the galatine can be cut in slices and arranged on a number of dishes, if for a large party. In that case, place a little jelly in the centre of each slice, and garnish the border of the dish with jelly and parsley. The time and materials given are for a turkey weighing about nine pounds. Any kind of fowl or bird can be prepared in the same manner.

To make the jelly: Draw forward the kettle in which the turkey was cooked, and boil the contents rapidly for one hour. Strain, and put away to harden. In the morning scrape off all the fat and sediment. Put the jelly in a clean sauce-pan with the whites and shells of two eggs that have been beaten with four table-spoonfuls of cold water. Let this come to a boil, and set back where it will just simmer for twenty minutes. Strain through a napkin, and set away to harden.

Galatine of Veal.

Bone a breast of veal. Season well with salt and pepper. Treat the same as turkey, using, however, two pounds of boiled ham instead of the tongue. Cook four hours.

Chicken in Jelly.

For each pound of chicken, a pint of water. Clean the chicken, and put to boil. When it comes to a boil, skim carefully; and simmer gently until the meat is very tender--about an hour and a half. Take out the chicken, skin, and take all the flesh from the bones. Put the bones again in the liquor, and boil until the water is reduced one half. Strain, and set away to cool. Next morning skim off all the fat. Turn the jelly into a clean sauce-pan, carefully removing all the sediment; and to each quart of jelly add one-fourth of a package of gelatine (which has been soaked an hour in half a cupful of cold water), an onion, a stalk of celery, twelve pepper-corns, a small piece of mace, four cloves, the white and shell of one egg and salt and pepper to taste. Let it boil up; then set back where it will simmer twenty minutes. Strain the jelly through a napkin. In a three-pint mould put a layer of jelly about three-fourths of an inch deep. Set in ice water to harden. Have the chicken cut in long, thin strips, and well seasoned with salt and pepper; and when the jelly in the mould is hard, lay in the chicken, lightly, and cover with the liquid jelly, which should be cool, but not hard. Put away to harden. When ready to serve, dip the mould in warm water and then turn into the centre of a flat dish. Garnish with parsley, and, if you choose, with Tartare or mayonnaise sauce.

Chicken Chaud Froid.

Skin two chickens, and cut in small pieces as for serving. Wash, and put them in a stew-pan with enough white stock to cover, and one large onion, a clove, half a blade of mace, a bouquet of sweet herbs and half a table-spoonful of salt. Let this come to a boil; then skim carefully, and set back where it will simmer for one hour. Take up the chicken, and set the stew-pan where the stock will boil rapidly. Put three table-spoonfuls of butter in the frying-pan, and when it melts, stir in two table-spoonfuls of flour, and cook until smooth, but not brown. Stir this into the stock, of which there must be not more than a pint; add four table-spoonfuls of glaze, and boil up once. Taste to see if seasoned enough; if it is not, add more salt and pepper. Now add half a cupful of cream, and let boil up once more. Have the chicken in a deep dish. Pour this sauce on it, and set away to cool At serving time, have large slices of cold boiled sweet potatoes, fried in butter till a golden brown, handsomely arranged on a warm dish. On them place the chicken, which must be very cold. On each piece of the meat put a small teaspoonful of Tartare sauce. Heap the potatoes around the edge of the dish, garnish with parsley, and serve.

To Remove a Fillet from a Fowl or Bird.

Draw the skin off of the breast, and then run a sharp knife between the flesh and the ribs and breast-bone. You will in this way separate the two fillets from the body of the bird. The legs and wings of the largest birds and fowl can be boned, and stuffed with force-meat, and then prepared the same as, and served with, the fillet. The body of the bird can be used for soups. Fillets from all kinds of birds can be prepared the same as those from chickens.

Chicken Fillets, Larded and Breaded.

Lard the fillets, having four fine strips of pork for each one, and season with salt and pepper. Dip in beaten egg and in fine bread crumbs. Fry ten minutes in boiling fat. Serve on a hot dish with a spoonful of Tartare sauce on each.

Chicken Fillets, Braised.

Lard the fillets as for breading. For each one lay a slice of fat pork in the bottom of the braising pan, and on this a very small piece of onion. Dredge the fillets well with salt, pepper and flour, and place them on the pork and onion. Cover the pan, and set on the stove. Cook slowly half an hour; then add one pint of light stock or water and the bones of one of the chickens. Cover the pan, and place in a moderate oven for one hour, basting frequently with the gravy. If the gravy should cook away, add a little more stock or water, (there should be nearly a pint of it at the end of the hour). Take up the fillets, and drain; then cover them with soft butter, and dredge lightly with flour. Broil till a light brown. Serve on a hot dish with the sauce poured around. Or, they can be dressed on a mound of mashed potato, with a garnish of any green vegetable at the base, the sauce to be poured around it.

To make the sauce: Skim all the fat from the gravy in which the fillets were cooked. Cook one table-spoonful of butter and one heaping teaspoonful of flour together until a light brown; then add the gravy, and boil up once. Taste to see if seasoned enough, and strain.

Chicken Fillets, Sauté.

Flatten the fillets by pounding them lightly with the vegetable masher. Season with pepper and salt, and dredge well with flour. Put in the frying-pan one table-spoonful of butter for each fillet, and when hot, put the fillets in, and cook rather slowly twenty minutes. Brown on both sides. Take up, and keep hot while making the sauce. If there are six fillets, add two table-spoonfuls of butter to that remaining in the frying-pan, and when melted, stir in one table-spoonful of flour. Stir until it begins to brown slightly; then slowly add one and a half cupfuls of cold milk, stirring all the while. Let this boil one minute. Season with salt, pepper and, if you like, a little mustard. Fill the centre of a hot dish with green peas or mashed potatoes, against which rest the fillets; and pour the sauce around. Serve very hot.

Chicken Curry.

One chicken, weighing three pounds; three-fourths of a cupful of butter, two large onions, one heaping table-spoonful of curry powder, three tomatoes, or one cupful of the canned article, enough cayenne to cover a silver three-cent piece, salt, one cupful of milk. Put the butter and the onions, cut fine, on to cook. Stir all the while until brown; then put in the chicken, which has been cut in small pieces, the curry, tomatoes, salt and pepper. Stir well. Cover tightly, and let simmer one hour, stirring occasionally; then add the milk. Boil up once, and serve with boiled rice. This makes a very rich and hot curry, but for the real lover of the dish, none too much so.

Veal Curry.

Two pounds of veal, treated in the same manner, but cooked two hours. Mutton and lamb can be used in a like way.

Chicken Quenelles.

One large chicken or tender fowl, weighing about three pounds; six table-spoonfuls of butter, one table-spoonful of chopped salt pork, three eggs, one teaspoonful of onion juice, one of lemon juice, half a cupful of white stock or cream, one cupful of stale bread, one of new milk, and salt and pepper to taste. Skin the chicken, take all the flesh from the bones, and chop and pound *very* fine. Mix the pork with it, and rub through a flour sieve. Cook the bread and milk together for ten minutes, stirring often, to get smooth. Add this to the chicken, and then add the seasoning, stock or cream, yolks of eggs, one by one, and lastly the whites, which have been beaten to a stiff froth.

Cover the sides and bottom of a frying-pan with soft butter. Take two table-spoons and a bowl of boiling water. Dip one spoon in the water, and then fill it with force-meat, heaping it; then dip the other spoon in the hot water, and turn the contents of the first into it. This gives the *quenelle* the proper shape; and it should at once be slipped into the frying-pan. Continue the operation until all the meat is shaped. Cover the quenelles with white stock, boiling, and slightly salted, and cook gently twenty minutes. Take them up, and drain for a minute; then arrange on a border of mashed potatoes or fried bread. Pour a spoonful of either Bechamel, mushroom or olive sauce on each, and the remainder in the centre of the dish. Serve hot.

Chicken Quenelles, Stuffed.

Prepare the force-meat as for *quenelles*. Soak four table-spoonfuls of gelatine for one hour in cold water to cover. Put two table-spoonfuls of butter in a frying-pan, and when hot, add one table-spoonful of flour. Stir until smooth, but not brown; then gradually stir in one pint of cream. Add one table-spoonful of lemon juice, a speck of mace and plenty of salt and pepper. Cook for two minutes. Stir in the soaked gelatine, and remove from the fire. Into this sauce stir one pint and a half of cold chicken, cut *very* fine. Set away to cool. Butter eighteen small egg cups, and cover the sides and bottoms with a thick layer of the force-meat. Fill the centre with the prepared force-meat, which should be quite firm. Cover with chicken. Place the cups in a steamer and cover them with sheets of thick paper. Put on the cover of the steamer, and place upon a kettle of boiling water for half an hour. Do not let the water boil too rapidly. Take up, and put away to cool. When cold, dip the *quenelles* twice in beaten egg and in bread crumbs. Fry in boiling fat for three minutes. Serve hot with a garnish of stoned olives.

Chicken Quenelles, Breaded.

Prepare the *quenelles* as before, and when they have been boiled, drain, and let them grow cold. Dip in beaten egg and roll in bread crumbs; place in the frying basket and plunge into boiling fat. Cook three minutes. Serve with fried parsley or any kind of brown sauce.

Veal Quenelles.

One pound of clear veal, one cupful of white sauce, six table-spoonfuls of butter, one cupful of bread crumbs, one of milk, four eggs, salt, pepper, a slight grating of nutmeg and the juice of half a lemon. Make and use the same as chicken *quenelles*.

Chicken Pilau.

Cut a chicken into pieces the size you wish to serve at the table. Wash clean, and put in a stew-pan with about one-eighth of a pound of salt pork, which has been cut in small pieces. Cover with cold water, and boil gently until the chicken begins to grow tender, which will be in about an hour, unless the chicken is old. Season rather highly with salt and pepper, add three tea-cupfuls of rice, which has been picked and washed, and let boil thirty or forty minutes longer. There should be a good quart of liquor in the stew-pan when the rice is added. Care must be taken that it does not burn. Instead of chicken any kind of meat may be used.

Chicken Soufflé.

One pint of cooked chicken, finely chopped; one pint of cream sauce, four eggs, one teaspoonful of chopped parsley, one teaspoonful of onion juice, salt, pepper. Stir the chicken and seasoning into the boiling sauce. Cook two minutes. Add the yolks of the eggs, well beaten, and set away to cool. When cold, add the whites, beaten to a stiff froth. Turn into a buttered dish, and bake half an hour. Serve with mushroom or cream sauce. This dish must be served the moment it is baked. Any kind of delicate meat can be used, the *soufflé* taking the name of the meat of which it is made.

Fried Chicken.

Cut the chicken into six or eight pieces. Season well with salt and pepper. Dip in beaten egg and then in fine bread crumbs in which there is one teaspoonful of chopped parsley for every cupful of crumbs. Dip again in the egg and crumbs. Fry ten minutes in boiling fat. Cover the centre of a cold dish with Tartare sauce. Arrange the chicken on this, and garnish with a border of pickled beets. Or, it can be served with cream sauce.

Blanquette of Chicken.

One quart of cooked chicken, cut in delicate pieces; one large cupful of white stock, three table-spoonfuls of butter, a heaping table-spoonful of flour, one teaspoonful of lemon juice, one cupful of cream or milk, the yolks of four eggs, salt, pepper: Put the butter in the sauce-pan, and when hot, add the flour. Stir until smooth, but not brown. Add the stock, and cook two minutes; then add the seasoning and cream. As soon as this boils up, add the chicken. Cook ten minutes. Beat the yolks of the eggs with four table-spoonfuls of milk. Stir into the blanquette. Cook about half a minute longer. This can be served in a rice or potato border, in a *croûstade*, on a hot dish, or with a garnish of toasted or fried bread.

Blanquette of Veal and Ham.

Half a pint of boiled ham, one pint and a half of cooked veal, one pint of cream sauce, one teaspoonful of lemon juice, the yolks of two uncooked eggs, salt, pepper, two hard-boiled eggs. Have the veal and ham cut in delicate pieces, which add with the seasoning to the sauce. When it boils up, add the yolks, which have been beaten with four table-spoonfuls of milled Cook half a minute longer. Garnish with the hard-boiled eggs.

Salmis of Game,

Take the remains of a game dinner, say two or three grouse. Cut all the meat from the bones, in as handsome pieces as possible, and set aside. Break up the bones, and put on to boil with three pints of water and two cloves. Boil down to a pint and a half. Put three table-spoonfuls of butter and two onions, cut in slices, on to fry. Stir all the time until the onions begin to brown; then add two spoonfuls of flour, and stir until a rich dark brown. Strain the broth on this. Stir a minute, and add one teaspoonful of lemon juice and salt and pepper to taste; if you like, one table-spoonful of Leicestershire sauce, also. Add the cold game, and simmer fifteen minutes. Serve on slices of fried bread. Garnish with fried bread and parsley.

This dish can be varied by using different kinds of seasoning, and by serving sometimes with rice, and sometimes with mashed potatoes, for a border. Half a dozen mushrooms is a great addition to the dish, if added about five minutes before serving. A table-spoonful of curry powder, mixed with a little cold water, and stirred in with the other seasoning, will give a delicious curry of game. When curry is used, the rice border is the best of those mentioned above.

Game Cutlets à la Royale.

One quart of the tender parts of cold game, cut into dice; one generous pint of rich stock, one-third of a box of gelatine, one quart of any kind of force-meat, four cloves, one table-spoonful of onion juice, two of butter, one of flour, three eggs, one pint of bread or cracker crumbs, salt, pepper. Soak the gelatine for one hour in half a cupful of cold water. Put the butter in a frying-pan, and when hot, add the flour. Stir until smooth and brown, and add the stock and seasoning. Simmer ten minutes; strain upon the game, and simmer fifteen minutes longer. Beat an egg and add to the gelatine. Stir this into the game and sauce and take from the fire instantly. Place the stew-pan in a basin of cold water, and stir until it begins to cool; then turn the mixture into a shallow baking pan, having it about an inch thick. Set on the ice to harden. When hard, cut into cutlet-shaped pieces with a knife that has been dipped in hot water. When all the mixture is cut, put the pan in another of warm water for half a minute. This will loosen the cutlets from the bottom of the pan. Take them out carefully, cover every part of each cutlet with force-meat, and set on ice until near serving time. When ready to cook them, beat the two eggs with a spoon. Cover the cutlets with this and the crumbs. Place a few at a time in the frying basket, and plunge them into boiling fat. Fry two minutes. Drain, and place on brown paper until all are cooked. Arrange them in a circle on a hot dish. Pour mushroom sauce in the centre, garnish with parsley, and serve. Poultry cutlets can be prepared and served in the same way.

Cutlets à la Duchesse.

Two pounds of Lamb, mutton or veal cutlets, one large cupful of cream, one table-spoonful of onion juice, four table-Spoonfuls of butter, one of flour, two whole eggs, the yolks of four more, two table-spoonfuls of finely-chopped ham, one of lemon juice and salt and pepper to taste. Put two table-spoonfuls of the butter in the frying-pan. Season the cutlets with salt and pepper, and when the butter is hot, put them in it. Fry gently for five minutes, if lamb or mutton, but if veal, put a cover on the pan, and fry very slowly for fifteen minutes. Set away to cool. Put the remainder of the butter in a small frying-pan, and when hot, stir in the flour. Cook one minute, stirring all the time, and being careful not to brown. Stir in the cream. Have the ham, the yolks of eggs and the onion and lemon juice beaten together. Stir this mixture into the boiling sauce. Stir for about one minute, and remove from the fire. Season well with pepper and salt. Dip the cutlets in this sauce, being careful to cover every part, and set away to cool. When cold, dip them in beaten egg and in bread crumbs. Fry in boiling fat for one minute. Arrange them in a circle on a hot dish, and have green peas in the centre and cream sauce poured around.

Cutlets served in Papillotes.

Fold and cut half sheets of thick white paper, about the size of commercial note, so that when opened they will be heart-shaped. Dip them in melted butter and set aside. After trimming all the fat from lamb or mutton chops, season them with pepper and salt. Put three table-spoonfuls of butter in the frying pan, and when melted, lay in the chops, and cook slowly for fifteen minutes. Add one teaspoonful of finely-chopped parsley, one teaspoonful of lemon juice and one table-spoonful of Halford sauce. Dredge with one heaping table-spoonful of flour, and cook quickly five minutes longer. Take up the cutlets, and add to the sauce in the pan four table-spoonfuls of glaze and four of water. Stir until the glaze is melted, and set away to cool. When the sauce is cold, spread it on the cutlets. Now place these, one by one, on one side of the papers, having the bones turned toward the centre. Fold the papers and carefully turn in the edges. When all are done, place them in a pan, and put into a moderate oven for ten minutes; then place them in a circle, and fill the centre of the dish with thin fried, or French fried, potatoes. Serve very hot. The quantities given above are for six cutlets.

Veal Cutlets with White Sauce.

One and a half pounds of cutlets, two table-spoonfuls of butter, a slice of carrot and a small slice of onion. Put the butter and the vegetables, cut fine, in a sauce-pan. Season the cutlets with salt and pepper, and lay them on the butter and vegetables. Cover tightly, and cook slowly for half an hour; then take out, and dip in egg and bread crumbs, and fry in boiling fat till a golden brown. Or, dip the cutlets in soil butter and then in flour, and broil. Serve with white sauce poured around. Put a quart of green peas, or points of asparagus, in the centre of the dish, and arrange the cutlets around them. Pour on the sauce. This gives a handsome dish. Or, serve with olive sauce.

Mutton Cutlets, Crumbed.

Season French chops with salt and pepper, dip them in melted butter, and roll in *fine* bread crumbs. Broil for eight minutes over a fire not too bright, as the crumbs burn easily. Serve with potato balls heaped in the centre of the dish.

www.ingramcontent.com/pod-product-compliance
Lightning Source LLC
Chambersburg PA
CBHW081626100526
44590CB00021B/3621